WAX
&
GOLD

ሰምና ወርቅ

WAX
&
GOLD
ሰምና ወርቅ

JOURNEYS in ETHIOPIA
& OTHER ROADS LESS TRAVELLED

SAM McMANUS

'M' Publishing House Ltd

First published worldwide by 'M' Publishing House Ltd, 2021

In partnership with:

Yellow Wood
Adventures

yellowwoodadventures.com

Paperback ISBN: 978-1-8384937-0-7
eBook ISBN: 978-1-8384937-1-4

Edited by Sarah Marshall

Cover design & maps by David Doyle at studiofree.co.uk

Photo of author by Sandra Solares at Insta: @brumaonblack

Design and production by Catherine Williams
at chapter-one-book-production.co.uk

Printed in the United Kingdom

To my father:

Edward Joseph McManus

CONTENTS

MAP OF ETHIOPIA

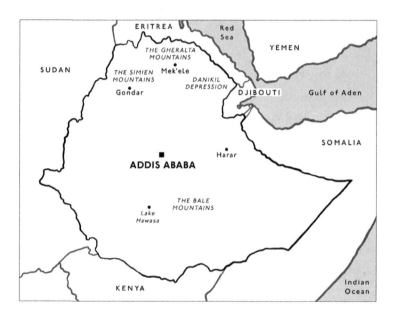

CULTURAL REGIONS OF ETHIOPIA

I

PROLOGUE:
A YELLOW WOOD

Two roads diverged in a yellow wood,
... and I—
I took the one less traveled by,
And that has made all the difference.

– from *The Road Not Taken* by **Robert Frost**

The most prized form of Ethiopian Amharic prose and poetry, loosely translated as 'wax and gold' ሰምና ወርቅ [sam-enna warq], is meticulously comprised with a focus on the duality of its meanings. The surface meaning, the wax, must be stripped away to reveal the hidden core of gold underneath. It also refers to Ethiopian Amhara culture and the traditional goldsmith's technique of making a clay mould around a wax model, draining the wax, and then pouring the molten gold into that mould.

In Amharic poetry, the phrase has come to signify the hidden, often spiritual meaning (the gold) beneath the apparent meaning (the wax) of the language: Once the ሰም [sam] is removed, the ወርቅ [warq] can be appreciated. In this same way the allure of Ethiopia encourages you to look deeper within yourself, to fully understand and appreciate a deeply rich spiritual significance, that often resonates beneath simple or plain exteriors.

In a similar vein, my travel writing tutor at university once told me that there must be two concurrent journeys taking place in good travel writing; the more obvious physical journey of the traveller, and then their inner, mental and spiritual journey. This collection of travel stories, compiled over a 15-year period, traces the character arc of my own life; from first discovering my deep love of travel, to moving away from it to a job that I despised and was destroying the planet, to renouncing this, and returning to a life in which I find both meaning and purpose, to help regenerate that natural world I hold so dear.

I have always instinctively felt more comfortable and at peace in the wild, natural environments of the world, and many of the stories here are simple accounts of my adventures and misadventures in seeking them out. I was interested in Kung Fu as a teenager and studied for a number of years under a genuine Chinese Shaolin Monk called Yang, who had somehow made his way from China to Tunbridge Wells in the patchwork quilt of fields, woods and farms in Kent in South East England, under what may or may not have been somewhat dubious circumstances.

I saved up money after finishing school when I was 18 years old by physical labouring on a building site, and paid for a year to attend a Shaolin Kung Fu monastery in the Northern Chinese province of Jilin. My grandfather insisted on me taking lots of books with me as although I was not a great reader, he said this would change, and promptly filled my backpack with Zola, Cervantes, Stendhal and Tolstoy. My sister also slipped in a notebook, the beginning pages filled with clippings from our favourite movies.

In my childhood bedroom at home a few weeks before my departure, I had a very vivid dream about being on a high hill next to a large gate with flags that had blown down. Fast forwarding to my first fight in China, me now with a shaved head and wearing orange pyjamas; my opponent was a huge Dutchman standing before me on an uneven flagstone platform in front of the monastery, perched on a high hill overlooking sodden rice fields. There had been a raging storm the night before and the entrance gate including its frame with the monastery flags had blown down. It was exactly the same as in my dream. At the very moment that I realised this, my opponent kicked me in the jaw and the fight began. I lost that fight.

Later I had terrible pains in my head so the monks sent for an elderly Chinese medicine man from one of the villages. He had a long white beard yet was brimming with vitality. By sticking acupuncture needles in my temples and in hands at the thumb joint, the pain was miraculously relieved. I left the monastery after just four months, however, and with my refunded money travelled around Southeast Asia. So, travelling for me really started accidentally. I was smoking a cigarette in a treehouse in North Thailand when I received a birthday card from my father, in which he wrote as a joke: "Happy 19th Birthday, it reminds me of when I was your age and climbed Mount Everest." I impulsively bought a flight via Bangladesh to Kathmandu and spent a month hiking in the Himalayas of Nepal.

I had never seen anything like it. I camped for two nights on Kala Patthar Mountain overlooking Everest, tucked into my minus-20 degrees down feather sleeping bag behind a dry-stone wall windbreak. At sunset one evening the sky turned a perfect shade of bright purple I have never seen before or since. Everest was the last thing the sun hit and for a precious few seconds, it shone a perfect gold, emblazoned against a backdrop of white ice and purple sky. I have been obsessed with travel and been chasing this particular dragon ever since. It would be fair to say that nearly every decision I took from that moment onwards was always weighted in favour of how much it would afford me the opportunity to travel.

The story *Festival in the Ryukyu Islands of Japan (2005)* recounts a time when I was on an exchange programme from my university in Bath, UK, studying English Literature, spending my second year living in Kyushu, Japan, studying Japanese. It was the first time I had spent this long in a foreign country and tried to integrate myself into a new culture and language. This story is about the extremes of this – both of the loneliness and excitement it involves. After graduating from university, I saved up money working in London and purchased a one-way ticket to South America. I was very idealistic and really believed that going back to nature and living in a traditional way was better than the modern world.

The story *The Jungle in Bolivia (2007)* is about both the majesty of the natural world, but also my sharp wake-up-call upon being confronted with the reality of the hardship and suffering of people living hand-to-mouth. After six months travelling up the west coast of Central America, I lived in Mexico for one year on the Pacific coast, before returning to the UK. After working for two years in London and two years in Dubai for financial media companies, I then returned to London to work for an oil & gas consultancy, landing what I thought was a golden ticket job at the time.

I continued to embark on many personal adventures throughout this time. A three-week holiday trip to Nepal to hike the Annapurna Circuit with my girlfriend, turned out to be pivotal. I was trying to get back the magic of that first spontaneous trip I had done when I was 19, but it just wasn't the same. We found it to be overrun with tourists. When we went into the teahouses we were asked if I wanted pasta or pizza. I felt swindled out of a genuine experience and stupid that I had chosen to go somewhere everyone else went, and vowed never to make the same mistake again.

Then, on a business trip, recounted in *Cairo (2015)*, I realised I was in the midst of a slow but unrelenting degradation of the soul. The more I learned about the oil and gas industry, the more I realised how much it was wrecking the planet, and the more this made me feel depressed at a very deep level; every day I would wake up with a dark force pushing down on my mind. I disliked who I was becoming and would go through phases of heavy drinking then phases of extreme exercise, but nothing fixed it. I realised I needed to make a fundamental change so I quit my job. I had no plan, but in the same week I decided to found a travel company. I chose Ethiopia as my first destination, even though I hadn't been there before. A great portion of this book focusses on the narrative of this first three-month transformative journey, a major turning point in my life.

My Ethiopian adventures formed the nucleus of my travel company, YellowWood Adventures, and the writings on

Iran, Mongolia, Kyrgyzstan, Oman and Lebanon recount my research trips to these wonderful countries, and I have had the good fortune to return many times since. I treasure all of these experiences, yet cannot help feeling uneasy as I look back on all those flights in planes emitting CO2 into the atmosphere. Did I know better at the time? Yes, I did if I'm honest, but I did it anyway. Now I feel it is important to take responsibility for my actions that have directly impacted the planet, and to move forward with positive change, as a means of beginning to rectify them.

I do not feign to be ahead of the curve; I would say I am on the curve. YellowWood Adventures now plants trees to offset the carbon emitted by the flights of every client and guide, and we partner with local charities in every country we travel in, making sure we are positively helping to regenerate and positively influence the ecosystems and communities we travel through. If I have learnt anything on my journeys, it is that the grass is greener where you water it. The final chapter in this book is entitled *Costa Rica: A case study of ecotourism (2020)*. Faced with the global pandemic, I flew to the tropical Central American country for some much-needed time out.

Costa Rica has been a posterchild of ecotourism for decades; its sustainable tourism model conserving both the natural environment, whilst simultaneously improving the wellbeing of local communities and the economy of the country as a whole. I used this valuable time to study its successes, and reflect upon how these can be applied to our own business model, and indeed the rest of the world, to help prevent the devastating effects of climate change. As a historic warning, the following is taken from the Ethiopian Orthodox Mezmur songs ዘለሰኛ

[zelesengha] played on a *begena*, an Ethiopian ten-stringed instrument belonging to the family of the lyre. Mezmur songs often include the wax and gold format to praise God and talk about hard times:

ከምድር ፈተና ከራብ ከስደቱ
እኛንስ የጎዳን ካለHC መቅረቱ

**More than the obstacles of the earth;
from drought and migration;
What hurts us most is being left without a seed**

The face-value meaning of the song (the ሰም wax) is that 'more than the experienced droughts and problems, what hurts us is the loss of harvest and no seeds left for the next planting'. But the second deeper more profound meaning (the ወርቅ gold) comes from the play on words of HC [zer] which means 'seed' but also 'tribe' [ነገድ]. The deeper meaning to the song is therefore that it is a greater pain to have the tribe wiped out. Very much in the spirit of Ethiopia's wax & gold ሰምና ወርቅ poetic meaning, it is fair to say that it took me a while to develop an appropriate appreciation of Ethiopia. The beauties of the country, away from the more obvious grandeurs of the countryside, are of a subtler nature. Time was needed for me to slow down and adjust to a fundamentally different way of life, and the singular flavour of the country's romance.

Ethiopia can be difficult, prickly, cutting, ruthless, unforgiving, infuriating, stark, confused and complex. Yet, like a densely constructed novel exposing the fundamental contradictions of human nature, or, say, the bright plumage of a flowering cactus, when her treasures are revealed, they are all the more exceptional for the contrasts they manifest. Rarely do I open a book or read a travel article on Ethiopia that does not include the famous line from 18th century historian Edward Gibbon's masterwork *The History of the Decline and Fall of the Roman Empire*: "Encompassed on all sides by the enemies of their religion, the Ethiopians slept near a thousand years, forgetful of the world by whom they were forgotten." It still perfectly encapsulates what makes this land so unique, so much from ancient times still remaining.

Although the modern world now has a stable foothold in the cities of Ethiopia, when one ventures out to the interior, this thin veneer rapidly falls away, unveiling the unchanged soul of the nation. One memory illustrates this perfectly: A man and his young son were ploughing a terraced wheat field below their grass hut with two oxen. Their field on the edge of a small river, this fell away off the high plateau in a series of three waterfalls. Their plough had a small sharp metal tip lashed to its wooden triangular sides, the long beam and ploughman's handle comprised of bark-stripped eucalyptus. They wore a few items of Western clothing – a shirt and a raggedy pair of trousers, both in bare feet. Aside from these few tiny elements that have seeped in from the outside world, the scene was timeless.

I believe it is the search for this timelessness that continues to drive me to travel to the wilder corners of this world.

2

ETHIOPIA: FIRST IMPRESSIONS & LALIBELA (2015)

Don't catch a leopard by the tail,
but if you do, don't let it go.

– Ethiopian Proverb

In Addis Ababa, Ethiopia's capital, a female labourer shovelled cement onto the concrete mesh of a six-story building, one of many incomplete edifices breaking through the undulating waves of tin roofs that lap around a few modern hotels and skyscrapers, on their way to the foothills of the Entoto Mountains. Corrugated metal sheets fencing construction sites were painted in alternating green and yellow. A purple blossom fell on the road between busy lanes of traffic. At the UN building, security bollards were being painted blue. The thick latticework of an ancient acacia trees shaded embassy guards in aquamarine camouflage, lazy AK47s slung over their shoulders.

I glided above it all on the Chinese-built tram system, listening to the company's marketing video in English as rusty

9

trash-clogged rivers trickled below and car fumes filled the altitude-thin air with haze. I was staying in Addis with some acquaintances; Erica and Sarunas who were living in a comfortable compound in an upmarket neighborhood the city. I had met Erica a few years previously in Madrid. Both Americans, they worked for the US Peace Corps stationed in various parts of the country, had met, fallen in love and married, and were now finishing up their posting together in the capital.

But this convenience emerged as a somewhat double-edged sword. After living in Ethiopia for more than three years, they were both now tired, and impatiently looking forward to returning home in the coming weeks. As a result, I was peppered with the more negative aspects and anecdotes of their Ethiopian lives, such as the daily hassles for money on the streets and the sometimes passive-aggressive attitude toward foreigners; their jaded exasperations making my first impressions rather glum indeed.

The view from the flight the previous day had overpowered my sleep-deprived brain. It was daunting in its magnitude as verdant plains and huge lakes gave way to rising plateaus, checkered fields, villages with broccoli trees crawling up cliffs onto tabletop steppes, through which mountains tore away. It was all so vast. I had the peculiar sensation this was an unconquerable land. Which indeed it is, as it is one of only two countries in Africa (the other is Liberia) never to be colonized by foreign powers. Although it was largely occupied by Italy from 1935 for six years, until the Allied Forces helped to drive out Mussolini's troops. This was Africa alright, and after a long stint in Europe I was going to have to make some mental adjustments.

Erica offered to show me the two towns she had lived in,

which was also an opportunity for her to say her final farewells. I didn't particularly like the towns, but the journeys to both were mesmerizing. We left the capital on a good road through plains and terraced mountainsides of pastoral harvest scenery. As far as the eye could see, fields were flecked with pale fluffy-domed stacks of *teff* reaped by hand then threshed by livestock to release the fine grain used to make the *injera* flatbread served with every meal. The *teff* was piled into a huge fort with cattle, horses or donkeys driven around in a circle on the inside, pulling the walls down as they threshed the golden grass.

Men, women and children, draped in shammas of simple design, squatted in the fields using dull metal hand sickles to carefully lay the grass in neat piles, all facing the same way. Fields of sorghum swayed in the sunlight. Ethiopian farmers are highly industrious, and every visible square metre of arable land is cultivated. Their grass houses [*sarbait*] are round with dried dung walls or rectangular longhouses with two tied and folded summits of grass. Circular stone walls link the houses and a few trees, creating tiny hamlet compounds which cannot have changed in design for millennia. Tin has been introduced and is used for many roofs [*korkorobait*] which although more practical, are not as romantic in appearance.

Yellow and brown fields tumbled in scorched ripples towards rock-strewn rivers where children herded goats with thin poles. At first glance, circular, brightly painted churches appeared like Asian temples nestled in the eucalyptus groves. Eucalyptus is now unfortunately the dominant species in the country, introduced by Menelik II for construction of the then new capital Addis Ababa ['New Flower' in Amharic] founded in 1887. It has since spread across the country like wildfire and consumes a huge amount of the soil's moisture. Its acidic leaves, roots and branches also have the ability to discourage the growth of other plants by a process called allelopathy where biochemicals called allelotoxins are released to gain a competitive advantage for survival. The trees are undoubtedly pleasing in appearance however, as the younger shoots rise from a soft turquoise into a pale pink, releasing their delicate fragrance onto the breeze.

Mountains soared in a tortured splendour with ferocious chasms leading off into the distance, exaggerated like the backgrounds of religious paintings. One particularly enormous gorge cleft the entire landscape in two in the hinterland, as if God himself had drawn his sword across the country. It is a biblical landscape. Four women wrapped in dark shammas walked in single file to the river balancing wicker baskets on their heads, children played at hitting each other with long poles, the men bathed unashamedly naked.

The 'roadside-truck-stop' nowhere town of Debresina sits at 3200m in the lap of a small mountain. Erica greeted old friends and we sat in a coffeehouse comprised of a tin roof with curtain sides and a floor strewn with cut grass. The coffee [*buna*] was as delicious as the guidebooks will tell you. Perched on low schools, we enjoyed several sugary cups while a group of local men at the next table chewed *khat* leaves, its amphetamine-like properties giving a glossy shine to their eyes and a general air of indolence.

Debrabirhan didn't fare much better, albeit with one exception: Erica guided us to the famous *arake* bar on the outskirts of the larger town, down a cobbled street that smelled of shit leading to a vista that, in the fading light, resembled an Italian landscape from a Merchant Ivory film. We walked into a very large room with an earthen floor, wooden benches and tables skirting the walls. Many poor looking Ethiopians with sun-blackened faces – giving credence to the Greek origin of their name of 'burnt skin' – were draped in white cotton shammas. Small shot glasses in front of them spilled a light amber liquid onto the dark wood. Children ran about, two of them hiding behind an embroidered curtain.

The *arake* was 80% proof which I found hard to believe until I tried some. A shot was three Birr, which is roughly six cents US or four pence sterling. When you have taken your shot you either bang your glass down on the table indicating you want a refill, or turn it upside-down. I banged mine down so hard the first time by accident the whole place looked around and laughed. More of Erica's local friends joined us.

Mezemir Girma, who teaches at the local university, quoted Shakespeare to me and expounded on the five Sources of Knowledge, being, in an order the significance I didn't fully grasp: Experience, Authority, Logic, Religion and Scientific Inquiry. I had no idea what he was talking about. One of his previous students, Genet, an attractive 23-year-old girl with a bob haircut and a tight-fitting dress, sat next to me and was a delightful mixture of extreme religious piety and flirtation. A surly manager at the commercial bank who looked like a wrestler completed our party.

The walls were covered with images of Jesus and Mary with one huge mural of the carrying of the cross. This was complimented by an eclectic collection of paintings from an abstract artist who could have been commissioned by the War Office in 1945; images depicting a man leaning on a stick, a rock-hewn church in Lalibela, a retro fox, leopard and zebra. We moved on to a *tej* house with orange walls, drinking the honey-fermented strong wine [*tej*] from glass potion bottles and clapping to a local man who was dancing. It was explained to me that the unique round *tej* bottle with a thin neck was developed to reduce the smell escaping, which can become bad if the honey is left to ferment too long, distracting the drinker.

We finished the evening eating delicious hot fried goat *tibs* served on many layers of *injera* flatbread from communal round trays. One rips off a piece of the *injera* with ones fingers and uses this to grab hold of pieces of the meat *tibs* and a spicy orange powder called *mita-mita* which always makes you cough if you don't soak it into the food properly. The moment I had first decided to visit Ethiopia, I was sitting at my desk in my Richmond apartment in West London, as the lead-grated windows glowed in the soft light of a fading crimson autumn evening. I had quit my job that week, deciding to start a travel company.

I was also breaking up with my girlfriend. We had met in Senegal in West Africa when I was there on a surfing holiday. She, coincidentally like Erica and Sarunas, had been living and working there for three years for the US Peace Corps. We had later travelled around Morocco together and I had flown out to her family's cattle ranch in the American Midwest. She had since moved to London to study a Masters degree, but I was so mixed up inside I couldn't share myself properly with another person, and I was causing us both real pain. This only amplified my need to leave. I knew I needed to go somewhere wild, and somewhere big. I had previously read about Ethiopia in Paul Theroux's book *Dark Star Safari* which recounts a solo journey in his Sixties from Cairo to Cape Town. His descriptions of golden plateau and eucalyptus groves had surprised me, and for some reason came into my mind in that moment. I scoured my book-lined windowsills as the sun went down, but I couldn't find my copy, I must have given it away. The only thing I could dig-out was George MacDonald Fraser's *Flashman on the March*, which places the insufferable Flashman as the fictional protagonist in the historical setting of Napier's British military expedition to Ethiopia in 1867. I began to read it immediately, then ran a bath and carried on reading for the rest of the evening. When I had finished the lighthearted novel, I knew nothing more about Ethiopia, but my mind was made up. It's funny how it goes sometimes.

Back in Addis I was starting to feel claustrophobic in the city. My plans to start a travel company were off to a somewhat shaky start, as I was certainly having mixed feelings about the country during these first days. I had an Indian visa in my passport and considered making a break for Kashmir instead, but I saw in the news that fighting had resumed in the troubled region. I seriously considered fleeing to Patagonia. 'No!', I told myself, I had only seen some of the capital city and nearby towns. I needed to give the country a chance, so I shouldered my backpack, made my farewells to my kind hosts, and caught a bus departing from Mescal Square at 5:00am, heading north to Ethiopia's touristic jewel in the crown: The UNESCO World Heritage site of the eleven 13th Century rock-hewn churches of Lalibela.

One thousand years ago, as King Lalibela lay in a poison-induced coma at the hand of his brother, he journeyed to Heaven where the angels commanded that he build a New

Jerusalem in Africa's then bulwark of Christianity as Ethiopia was the second country in the world to declare itself Christian (after Armenia). His stonemasons cut directly down into the living rock of mountainsides to achieve this, the church roofs therefore remaining at ground level.

Standing in the dimly lit caverns with my hand pressed against the cold, rough surface of a pillar, I could feel I was touching part of the natural world where men and women shouldn't really be. The eleven churches are not as finely carved as the cathedrals of Europe, nor do they hold the eye like the lines of the architects of Greece, and yet, sitting alone in the presence of these monoliths, I felt the force of time creep upon me quietly, like a whisper. It was as confusing as an un-remembered memory or the brief grasp of a language we do not understand. All at once it was whisked away and forgotten, and I was left blinking in the bright light of day.

Walking between the huge metre-thick pillars of Biete Medhane Alem church, [*Biete* means 'House of' similar to the Arabic *Bayt* and *Medhane Alem* means 'The Saviour of the World'] the air cool and clammy, there was a sudden power cut. I was left alone with two priests reclining on the floor by the parapet and a man praying in one of the corners of the giant edifice. An atmosphere of peace and holiness emanated from the walls. Months later, I relayed this experience to an Ethiopian called Sammie on the balcony of the Sheraton Hotel in Addis.

"Ah yes," he had replied, "you can actually *feel* it."

I continued to explore in the semi-darkness. Sanctuaries containing the Holy of Holies were hidden from view by huge curtains hanging on weak aluminum poles. It is here the Tabot is held, a replica of the Ark of the Covenant which the holds the tablets on which the Biblical Ten Commandments were inscribed, and where God's presence appears in the church. The cheap fabric was patterned in gaudy, shiny spots or a 1970s rose-print; the shoddiness was somehow endearing, being of so little importance within the grandeur of the setting.

Men and women in cream robes sat around in circles on the floor eating, their cleft prayer sticks lying around at all angles. Power cables hung through windows carved into the stone in the shape of an ancient swastika. This symbol originates from the deepest, darkest history of India and Persia, although its arms facing in the other direction to that used by the German Nazi party, and has always symbolized 'peace'. An 800-year-old olive wood chest had its missing front section replaced with plywood. The worn floors were covered with cheap carpets and with the power restored, thin neon-tubed lighting made the smooth sections of the walls ripple like mercury.

Candles flickered. Some of the ceilings were painted in tribal patterns and someone somewhere was beating a drum. Subterranean tunnels led to the other ten churches, past endless caves of odd sizes and indefinable purpose. A priest sporting a white turban and rolled-up umbrella, emerged to open a locked door and let us inside Biete Amanuel, the private chapel of the royal family. It is the finest example of the perfectly symmetrical Aksumite design. Sculptors carved stone to represent wooden beams below a vaulted, cracked ceiling. Sacred bees buzzed in their hive high up behind a small wooden door in the vertical walls of the rock courtyard.

Biete Abba Libanos [House of Abbot Libanos] is hewn directly out from the strata of a cliff. I entered to find red carpets, benches and large hide drums laid around its cavernous perimeter. A light bulb hung from a thin cable emitting a soft radiance. Frescoes and framed icons featured Ethiopian faces painted in bright colours; shapes and bodies occasionally merged into each other for no reason. There were many unexpected elements to European Christian eyes: when Saint George slays a dragon, there is an unexplained woman tied to a tree; apostles are depicted as Persian kings; soldiers with dog heads carry spears; God [Abou] wears a cloak of feathers and is flanked by lions and leopards.

The priests chant in the ancient language of *Ge'ez* which nearly all those outside of the clergy do not understand, similar to the Latin spoken by priests in Europe. I sat and watched the sun set over the great cross-shaped church of Bete Giyorgis [House of Saint George] hewn out from the mountainside before me. The jarring sensations of my first days and accompanying worries were starting to slip from my shoulders. Maybe I was onto something after all.

3

FESTIVAL IN THE RYUKYU
ISLANDS OF JAPAN (2005)

I had spent six months studying Japanese at a sleepy Kyushu university, the most southern of the four main islands of Japan. Set amid bamboo-forested mountains, it was a far cry from the neon jungle of Tokyo. I eagerly awaited the coming two months of Spring Holiday to interrupt the growing malaise of settlement, and wished to put some of my hard-earned vocabulary to the test on the road. Packing a tent and battered gas cooker into my rucksack, I shouldered my surfboard case and caught a train down to the southernmost port of Kagoshima. Smoke exuded lazily from the strata volcano on Sakurajima [cherry blossom island] as the ship's funnel threw sparks out into the pale blue sky. I sat on the portside eating Ritz Biscuits.

When the world was still young and floating like oil, the gods Izanagi and Izanami thrust a spear into the sea. The brine that dripped from the spear became an island upon which the two performed a marriage rite around a pillar, and built their home. Izanami, the female god, then gave birth to the other islands of Japan, and also their deities known as *kami*. The little-known Ryukyu Islands spread from the four main islands in a perfect half-moon-shaped archipelago south for 1050 kilometres, all the way down to Taiwan. Okinawa is the central pendant in this delicate chain of lost gemstones, set in the turquoise East China Sea.

The tips of volcanic, submarine mountains, the islands abound in coral reefs and subtropical vegetation. Once their own proud kingdom, they traded from Java to Japan, China and Korea, exporting sugar cane, sweet potatoes, guava, papaya and tobacco, flourishing in tradition and wealth. The region was formally annexed to Japan by the Meiji government in 1879, the monarchy abolished, and the Japanese language introduced as standard. After years of vassalage whereby sword owner-ship was prohibited, this is where the martial art of karate originates from.

Tanegashima – 456 km sq – pop; approx. 36000

In 1543 Mendez Pinto, a Portuguese merchant travelling from China, introduced muskets into the island, the first time they had ever entered Japan. The name of the island has come to mean 'firearm' in Japanese and not ironically, it is now home to Japan's largest space centre, established in 1969. I camped on the east coast for a few days as set after set of neat, glossy and highly surfable waves rolled into shore. Grey boulders had tumbled out into the sea protecting the great roots of a gnarled tree that rose up amidst the sea mist.

I took a bus to the south of the island, and being the only passenger, sat up front talking to the driver in broken sentences.

His skin was brown and creased like greaseproof paper. He wore a small pilot's cap at a jaunty angle. We passed a razor wire fence and a large sign, the white paint of a space shuttle flaking off in the sun. Strange aluminum shapes and tall red-painted masts bobbed and winked over grassy ridges. Hugging the west coast, the road meandered down and the tall mountains and ancient forested mountains of Yakushima rose out from the sea in the near distance in a grey haze. The driver was born on Tanegashima and had been driving buses there since he was eighteen. Now approaching sixty, I asked him what it was like on Yakushima. Slipping me an enigmatic wink, he boastfully replied that he had never been there.

Yakushima – 505 km sq – pop; approx.14000

Yakushima is home to some 1,900 species and subspecies of rich flora, many being unique in the region. A rude pentagon from the sky, the mountains form a crown of stone protecting the basin of ancient forest within from the outside world. Natural hot springs called *onsen* pepper the coast where it is customary to bathe naked. I passed over a metal drawbridge that spanned a gushing river and the mountain trail plunged into a murky boscage of pre-historic jungle. A fine carpet of olive moss covered the immoveable rocks and decaying logs. Sinewy vines and branches criss-crossed the glowing jade light from the canopy in leafy capillaries. I experienced a feeling of infinite antiquity and calm.

Great trunks of umber wood rose up towards the sky, the thick bark pitted like termite hills, dusted in a fine malachite green fungus that lightly brushed off onto your hand. Wild deer acknowledged me without interest. An ancient stump approximately fifteen feet in diameter was completely hollow, inside incense burned at a small wooden shrine to the gods of the forest. Higher up, vistas of peaks spread out in all directions, one was grassy with pale grey boulders interspaced like pebbles in a rippling stream. The rain came down in great globules completely soaking me and my pack. I stayed in mountain huts for two nights, miraculously finding a small box of candles with which to dry out a few clothes.

I met a couple on their honeymoon and after some shared food and lengthy enquiries from me concerning their map for conversation's sake (I had one in my rucksack), we parted and they seemed thrilled to have met a foreigner. Most of the Japanese had matching fluorescent waterproof jackets and trousers. At one particularly beautiful part of the forest where the *sugi* (cedar) had a deep amber bark, I became stuck behind a tour group, watching as the red, purple, pink and blue spacemen navigated the foliage in small steps for mankind. The *jomon sugi*, dated at approximately 7000 years old, is the most ancient cedar tree in the world.

Miyakojima – 158.70 km sq – pop; approx. 56.200

On the overnight boat everyone slept on the floor in rows with small mats and tough pillows. In the morning uninhabited islands crawled by like slugs in the drizzle outside. Children leaped and scuffled over their reclining grandmother like young cubs. The boat stopped for about four hours to transfer mail and supplies.

Okinawa Island - 1201.03 km sq - pop; approx 1.2 million

From late March through to June 1945, the Battle of Okinawa or *Tetsu no Ame* [The Rain of Steel] raged unceasingly with the most appalling loss of life. As the US troops gained occupation, Japanese soldiers and civilians alike leapt from the southern cliffs onto the reef in their thousands both through fear of the invaders, and to preserve their honour rather than surrender. Now approximately 25,000 American military personnel with an equal number of American civilian employees are stationed in Okinawa. The local people continue to resent this overwhelming presence. I camped near a memorial park at the 'Suicide Cliffs' where the jagged reef, abandoning the subtropical vegetation, marches out into the ocean and plunges down into the crystal waters.

The Ryukyu family graves dotted the countryside. Their enormous rounded concrete roofs splayed out at the sides like the shells of giant dead turtles. I met a local Japanese surfer called Hibiki in an internet café and ended up staying at his flat for a week, just two minutes from Sunabe's graffiti clad concrete harbor and reef break, where we surfed most days as US Air Force jets screamed overhead.

Hibiki almost broke his leg after losing the key to his flat and trying to climb in through the third storey window.

The following morning we were cornered by his elderly landlady and ushered into her ground floor apartment for a cup of green tea. Her husband ambled into the room, one side of his body completely paralyzed. He looked at me with bleary, yellowing eyes and told me very slowly that when he was young he had served in the Japanese navy and seen the bomb detonate whilst on a ship off the coast of Nagasaki.

Ishigakijima – 228.91 km sq – pop; approx. 43,770

Plantations of pineapples, sugar cane and papayas broke up the landscape in uneven shapes and shades of green. I weighed down the corner of the tent with rocks on the utterly deserted beach and it rained for four days. On the fifth day I woke up and it wasn't raining. I washed in the stream and cursed myself for over-sleeping and missing the early morning waves. I was so tired the night before I had forgotten to set my alarm. The beach I was camping on was wild and scattered with coral. Further inland the trees had wavy trunks that resembled plumes of smoke from a fire.

The sky was a bright blue I hadn't seen for days. After cleaning my teeth, I stood naked in the stream and let the sun rest on my body. Out at sea, freighters drifted along. I had felt lonely camping on this beach. I walked gingerly to my tent (I had cleared the rocks, coral and creepers to pitch it) and slipped on some shorts. I took my knife and a coconut I had found washed up the day before. I had sharpened the blade recently and it cut into the husk smoothly as I ripped it off. My wrist was still hurting like hell from a surfing injury, so I tightened the bind with my teeth. I pierced one of the three weak spots on the top of the nut and tipped it up to drink the milk.

Rancid fluid filled my mouth, bitter with the taste of decay and faintly blue in colour. I spat it out, cursed, and hurled the nut down the beach. Shell crabs scuttled around pieces of onion, discarded from one of my previous meals. Wearing their shells like lop-sided berets, they really did look like drunks, I thought to myself. I went through the routine of packing up camp, and in about twenty minutes, I'd slid my board into its case, shouldered my bag and set off up the beach. It felt good to have trainers on, and I took pleasure in crushing the coral mercilessly beneath me. I scrambled up a thin, slippery path through the steep jungle; pack digging into my shoulders, board clumsy and awkward.

Huge great leaves, sometimes three-feet-long, were still dripping with moisture. The light came down in shafts, with occasional glimpses of the blue ocean. I finally reached the road and headed for a bridge crossing a large ravine. I followed the road for about an hour. Now and then cars passed but I didn't want a lift. I was happy walking. I set my pack down and stared blankly at a road sign map, but I didn't understand the kanji. A small white van approached, and I stuck my arm out. He stopped beside me, and the farmer offered me a lift.

I went through the usual routine of explaining where I was from, what I was doing in Japan, and I asked him about his farm. He had very brown tough-looking hands and big widely spaced teeth. I gave him a wave after he dropped me off. I headed to the surf shop in town where I knew the pretty shop assistant wouldn't mind if I left my board there for a day or two. I chatted to her for a bit, but ever since I told her I was 21, she had treated me differently. She was 26. I thanked her, went to the dock and bought a ticket for Kuroshima.

The dock was bustling with people: farmers and old women, small families – all wearing simple and often dirty clothes. One man wore a suit, but you could see his body move underneath and the symbol was lost. Just a poor man. The boats were small with powerful engines and could hold about 40 people. They looked a bit like spaceships but 'star cruisers' sounded better. I walked through to the back of my boat where there were four shabby benches and I chose the one furthest. The engines roared and whined below me. A few men came out to smoke cigarettes and I was glad for the noise as I didn't feel like talking.

Kuroshima – 10.2 km sq – pop; approx. 230, over 3000 cows

I found rough constructions for the festival the following day and looked for a good place to camp. I pitched camp next to a wide tree with large crevices at the base where I could put things. I boiled some water over my tiny gas cooker in one of the hollows of the tree and cooked up some soba. When it was done, I took it off and placed my pan over the heat and threw in the last of my meat, onions, large Japanese cabbage and *enoki* – a delicious small mushroom. On second thoughts, I put in a lot more spice as I knew the meat wouldn't last another day. When it was cooked up, I took it down to the beach and ate in the dark and washed up in the sea.

I dried my feet as best as I could, lay on my sleeping bag and zipped up the mosquito net. For one reason or another I slept very badly that night. My mind went back to lots of places I had been and people I had met, and I thought about my friends back home. This was now the longest time I had spent in a foreign country, trying to integrate myself into a new culture and language. There are extremes to this – both in terms of the excitement and loneliness it involves.

I awoke to the sound of rain on the tent. I checked the time.

It was 9.20am, and the festival didn't start until 10. "I'll be damned if I'm going out in this," I thought, stubbornly picking up my book. Soon the rain eased off, and I went down to the sea to wash. The wind was biting, so I was surprised at how warm the water was, but I couldn't fully wash as there was a man in a raincoat with a fishing rod and I didn't want to offend him. I was aware that everything I had (including myself) was rather dirty and needed a good clean. It was about a week since I had last been to a hostel in Okinawa. I went back to my tent in the drizzle and dressed in muddy jeans, trainers, T-shirt and jumper. At that moment I was rather bored with camping.

I could hear noises from the festival, so I headed that way feeling vaguely embarrassed about my appearance. I entered a large muddy area. All around the edges, stalls had been set up and there was a big stage hosting the world's worst production of 'Power Rangers' with the superhero fighting a dragon. His comrades consisted of a pig and two cows with oversized heads. The action music and explosion sounds beat into my head. It was too loud to ignore. At least I didn't have to worry about my clothes – everyone was muddy and wearing rain macs. Oh dear, I thought to myself, this might turn out to be rather dull.

I took a walk around the stalls, all selling roasted cow and alcohol. I ordered rare beef, garlic bread and a glass of red wine for breakfast. The sky was grey and completely overcast. After a seemingly endless losing battle, the power ranger was victorious due to some amazing secret advice from the pig; and after much arm swinging, explosions and fighting his foe was vanquished. I gulped down some more cow, feeling somewhat demoralized. A healthy-looking chap in a red jacket caught my eye and raised his glass. "Kampai!" We touched glasses and drank. The group immediately turned to me for the usual round of questions. I explained I was a student, and they congratulated me on my basic Japanese.

There was a woman not yet 40 in a black jacket with rather grey gums, a nice face and a red stud in each ear. The man standing next to me had a coat done up all the way to his chin and a round hat pulled down low, the brim floppy in the wet. It reminded me of something an SAS frogman might wear. I was taller than everyone of course. I found out that they were from different parts of the country, but now lived on the neighbouring island of Iliomotejima. They were all drinking *shouchu*, a clear, strong alcohol in plastic cups.

The lady in the black jacket asked me if I liked *shouchu*, and I replied that I liked it immensely and preferred it hot. She promptly returned with a cup for me and some more for others. I thought this was surprisingly generous. "Oh don't worry; its free," she replied. Maybe this wouldn't be so bad after all. I drained my glass and was offered another. The hot alcohol in my belly felt good and I felt my spirits lighten. A man with large limbs and long, loping movements came towards me. He had a pronounced jaw and a scraggily mop of black hair. He put down the young boy he was carrying on his shoulders.

I shook his hand, and he asked my name. Everyone then told me their names which I immediately forgot. In Japan, when someone tells me their name, the chances are slim that I'd heard it before, so it becomes a new word to be learned. Instead of awkwardly making everyone repeat them several times I just give up. I picked up the kid and gave him a shake and he giggled. Then I lifted him up and put him on my shoulders.

Two more men joined the small group. They were young

and looked fit. I found out they both worked as rice farmers. The first had a wide, easy smile with strong teeth and longish hair down over his forehead. His name was Yuki. I remembered it because it was the name of an American friend's girlfriend back in Kyushu. The other man had long curly dark black hair and was wearing a white T-shirt and striped jacket. In my mind I called him Joseph, but never asked again to learn his real name. Oddly, he had bare feet, although everyone else was wearing wellies.

They were drinking fast and encouraged me to join them. I forgot about the grey, drizzly weather. My Japanese became more animated. They were all very interested to hear about England. When you call Kent the 'Garden of England' it sounds rather grand. A recent word I had learnt was *mokuzai*, which means 'to be made from wood'. I went into a rather long narration about how castles in England were always made from stone but that in Japan they are always made from wood and so tend to burn down, so that's why castles in England are always older. I was rambling but they were listening, and I was just pleased to deftly slip in my new word; it's a battle of inches.

I put the boy down (whose name, Teru, I had now committed to memory) and slipped away to watch the show properly. Some boys dancing hip-hop style with white flannels tied round their heads. They weren't just good; they were brilliant. After them, some girls came on and did a sexy dance to more good music. I looked over at Yuki, he saw me and gave me a wide grin. I grinned back. A rock and roll band came on. Yuki, Joseph, the boy and his father came with me to the front after picking up some more booze on the way. It turned out Yuki and Joseph were more drunk than I had thought, hurling each other about and rolling in the mud. Teru was back on my shoulders and I was dancing.

Joseph kept stealing his wellies and throwing them away and I would chase after them and bend down so Teru could pick them up. It was a good game and soon he was whacking Joseph with his boots. Yuki did a great Klinsman slide in the mud and almost knocked over a television camera. I was glad I had met these guys. When the band had finished, we went back to our table to restock drinks and have a rest. When a more traditional band came on dressed in kimonos with drums and three-stringed shamisen everyone was back dancing again and we were soon also in the fray. Old women were waving their arms like a Hawain Hula, while lots of steaming cow soup was being passed around.

The people in front formed a line and all danced waving flags, flannels and anything they could get hold of. Lots of children were running about and they and some of the people were wearing cow hats with little horns and a smiling cow face. I decided I wanted to buy one for Teru, and we went running around to find the stall. Lots of people were sitting on the wet ground in circles, always bottles of the local strong drinks *shouchu* and Okinawan *awamori*, fermented from rice, in the middle with bright, flashing blue and yellow labels. We found the stall and bought a hat and cheap plastic watch. We went back and carried on dancing.

The next two hours were a blur of constant refills and back-slapping. Joseph gave me one of his cigarettes and it was so strong my head went spinning. The man in the SAS frogman hat told me he worked on a ship that netted black pearls. Some of them are worth £250, he said, but he was still poor. Yuki taught me how to say, "Eat shit and go to bed", and asked me if I knew how to swear in Japanese. I confidentially rolled off a string of obscenities dutifully memorized in Miyazaki and watched his eyes brighten with understanding and mirth. The audience was then pushed back with a rope to create a wide space for a giant cow with small horns draped with red cloth lined with gold. I thought they were going to kill it, but they had a tug of war instead, with six or seven Japanese always hopelessly dragged across the ground by the cow. I wanted to try but people had reserved their spaces in advance. Joseph and Yuki failed to do any better than the rest and Joseph cut his arm on the ground and had to go to the doctor and get a dressing. More shouchu, meat, mud and singing.

At last the inevitable happened: the stall stopped serving alcohol. This was a good time to leave and I said my goodbyes. The woman with the red earrings was Teru's mother. She wrote down her address and asked me to come and visit them on the neighbouring Iliomotejima, and I did indeed later visit and spend time with the family. I shook many hands and weaved my way back to my tent. I packed up my wet things and headed for the dock. Suddenly I was exhausted. I bought a ticket and slept all the way back on the boat. I found a hostel, dumped my stuff in the dorm and collapsed into the shower. The hot water beat down on my head and I had a good wash.

I took off the binding, my wrist was still slightly swollen but it was getting better. I lay on my bed but couldn't go back to sleep, so I read for a few hours. I could hear some people in the hostel commune having a party, but I couldn't face new introductions. My body felt limp and I had reached an increasingly depressing point in my Somerset Maugham novel

Of Human Bondage (not what it sounds like), so I decided to go out. Slipping into my dirty clothes, I figured I would go to a *ramen yasan* [noodle bar].

I turned the corner and my fatigue left me instantly; it was as if a silk shroud had been pulled over me and had taken all my tiredness with it. "If that's not fate, I don't know what is!" I exclaimed. Yuki, Joseph, the big guy and some girls were stumbling towards me. We greeted each other enthusiastically and they told me they had just been saying it would have been good if I was with them. I figured they were too drunk to lie so quickly, but you never know. They had missed the last boat to Iliomotejima and were staying in town for the night and getting the first boat in the morning. I checked that Teru and his mum had also got a place to stay and they said they had and were asleep.

The girls left and I realised they were with a guy I had seen dancing earlier. He wore too-tight jeans that exposed womanly hips above a big marijuana buckle, a great big bone necklace around his neck and a sleazy moustache. I thought he was a complete dickhead. He was exceptionally drunk. We all piled into an *izakaya* and sat on tatami mats at big, long, low tables of dark wood. The sleazy guy was loud and annoying and started to harass some girls sitting at the next table. I told him to shut up and sit down. Fortunately, within 20 minutes he was so drunk he fell asleep in the corner and we didn't bother to wake him. "Eat shit and go to bed," I told him as he slept, and everyone laughed.

We had all sobered up a bit and felt relaxed and comfy. Outside it had started to rain again. I got out my notebook and various people taught me many new words; in exchange I taught them some English. I told them how me and my friends would toast each other with three clinks: the top of the glass, the bottom and then the whole lot. "Never above, never below, always the same". We talked until the place closed, finishing with a steaming hot bowl of *soba* each. After eating the noodles, we lay down our chopsticks and drunk the hot oily soup from the bowl with our hands. Time to leave, quick goodbyes, Yuki gave me his address. We only woke up the sleeping guy so he would pay his share.

I had paid for two nights. I woke up with a terrible headache and lay in bed dozing for a few hours. It felt good to be in a bed. I went out and bought bacon and eggs and cooked them with bean sprouts and drank coffee. I went to the surf shop to get my board and talked to the girl for a bit. She was really was pretty, blessed with the effortless delicacy and grace of Japan. I asked her if she would come out with me on Thursday night and she said yes, but later cancelled. I sat around reading some surf magazines for a bit but left soon. When I'm tired language comes slow. Another night of luxury then back to the lonely beach with the good reef break. Silence. Rain.

4

ETHIOPIA: THE SIMIEN MOUNTAINS (2015)

Walking along a damp footpath between mossy rocks enclosed by lichen-covered trees, I emerged onto the *za'atar*-scented platform, the herb's fragrance transporting my mind back to the Middle East. With sheer drops on both sides, the ridge narrowed and fell away, tapering into a thin finger of stone pointing due north. Lilac, crimson and yellow flowers jittered in the breeze amongst thistles and other mountain foliage. Across the valley, four mountain peaks rose as a crown through the cloud and re-emerged below, falling in thin tree-lined ridges like the flying buttresses of a cathedral.

I was standing on the edge of what is essentially a one-sided Grand Canyon. The ridges led down to three tiny soft mounds of bright green barley fields sown by the inhabitants of the grass-roofed villages, before dropping swiftly down again into the huge cleft of an unseen river. Curved-horned ibex silently drifted across unnavigable, isolated battlements, bathed in shadow apart from a few patches of golden illumination.

This viewpoint was close to our third camp in the Simien Mountains, which is the most popular trekking destination in Ethiopia. After Lalibela this was the next obvious place to visit.

Five days previously, I had been milling around the castle town of Gondar trying to figure out the best way to view the Simien ['Northern' in Amharic] range. Many of the tour operators seemed overpriced for what they were offering. At the bar in my hotel I met two young men from Israel, Tal and Elad, who were having the same problem. After we had reviewed all the options open to us, we decided to organize our own expedition by hiring our own guide and bringing our own supplies, and immediately felt like our newfound plan required some sort of celebration.

By good fortune, that day was the Saint's day festival of *Mariyamn*, the Virgin Mary, and we caught one of the innumerable blue tuk-tuks known as *bajaj* to a neighbouring village. We were immediately greeted with fantastic scenes of celebration on the main street. Lined with colourful paper tassels, it was full of people laughing, chatting and dancing. We were invited into villagers' houses to drink huge beakers or old tins full to the brim of green millet-based beer *talla*, which has the exact colour and consistency of pond water. We had a great time playing with the children and mock-flirting with the young women who crowded around us, drinking cup for cup alongside their male counterparts.

Tal and Elad had heard that there was a Jewish cemetery just outside the village. After our third house party, we recruited some local children to guide us there, where we rested in the cool shade of a eucalyptus grove amongst blue and white painted tombs inscribed with the Star of David. The historical ties between Israel and Ethiopia are significant. In the 10th Century BC, the legendary Queen of Sheba, or Makeda, occupied kingdoms of Aksum in northern Ethiopia and Saba, centered around present-day Yemen.

She travelled to Jerusalem on what was most likely a trade mission to meet King Solomon "with a very great retinue, with camels bearing spices, and very much gold, and precious stones" (I Kings 10:2). After a large feast, she agreed to stay with Solomon in his palace if he promised not to do her any harm, which the king agreed to on the condition that she wouldn't steal from him. Versions of the story differ at this point: either as a consequence of spicy food or from having drunk too much alcohol, Makeda awoke with a great thirst and drank a cup of the king's water. Having broken her oath, she could not refuse a union with Solomon and upon her return journey home, bore him a son.

Solomon had given Makeda a ring as a token of faith and after her son, Menelik I, had grown up in Ethiopia, he travelled to Jerusalem bearing the ring to meet his father. He could not be persuaded to stay, however, and upon his return, he and his followers stole the Ark of the Covenant, which they brought back to Ethiopia. It is now said to reside in the Church of Our Lady Mary of Zion in Aksum. From Menelik I, the Solomonic dynasty continued to rule Ethiopia until 1974, when the last emperor, Haile Selassie, was deposed by the communist *Derg* regime. All of Ethiopia's kings and emperors from this Solomonic dynasty were from the Amhara people, whose territory includes the Simien Mountain range.

Ethiopian Jews, also known as *Beta Israel* or *falashas* (a derogatory term), also claimed descendance from Menelik I, although perhaps it is more likely that they emigrated south from Egypt after the first exile. From the 16th Century, Ethiopian Jews inhabited much of the Simien Mountains as, after centuries of warring with the Ethiopian Christian kingdoms, the latter rose to dominance and the *Beta Israel* withdrew into the more defensible mountain range. During the 20th Century, most Ethiopian Jews have resettled in Israel, creating a large community there.

The next morning, I got up early and went into the town, procuring a kerosene stove (I couldn't find any gas burners), water purification tablets, pots, a pan, plates and cutlery. I knew we would be employing locals for the park-enforced compulsory role of a scout, and also a driver for a mule we would need to carry our heavier supplies, so I bought a litre of the stiff alcohol *arake* which I knew would go down well with them during the cold evenings.

Dropping all this gear at the hotel, myself, Tal and Elad headed to the local market. This was a wonderful experience as we were somewhat of a novelty and greatly enjoyed bargaining loudly and ostentatiously for each and every item including potatoes, lentils, macaroni, rice, spaghetti, onions, garlic, chillies, cabbage, aubergine, spices, oil, coffee, dates, biscuits, chocolate, peanut butter and sardines, with sacks and string to load the mule. People would crowd around us as we alternatively yelled, commiserated, begged, cajoled and feigned mock outrage in front of huge sacks of fresh produce or open baskets of kaleidoscopically-coloured spices, laughing at our enthusiasm and ineffectiveness.

We headed up the town of Debark the following day to hire our guide and muleman. It is hard to find anything complimentary to write about Debark – it is basically a dump of a town you have to go through to get to the mountains. We went through the usual stress of finding and haggling rates to employ our local team, feeling like nothing more than walking ATMs in the well-established tourism machine. Eventually we set off in the early morning mist the following day, mule in tow loaded with our supplies, driven by a sprightly character named Mercabul Fared. Our scout was a somewhat downtrodden individual named Alemu Mereti. Wearing a flat cap and carrying a PPSH Soviet automatic rifle, date-stamped 1944 with Cyrillic lettering and about four bullets in the magazine, he had the aura of an Ethiopian Elmer Fudd.

The walk through golden *teff* fields was stunning and after a few steep climbs we reached the first viewpoint overlooking a vast precipice. The Simien Mountains fall away in a lethal drop to a long mountain-filled plateau that stretches as far as the eye can see. You are so high, regular-sized mountains look like sand dunes, only occasionally broken by *ambas* of towering rock but with table-flat tops, which for some reason reminded me of the Foreign Ministry Building in Cairo.

A dirt track road runs through the national park, used as a supply line for tourists who do not wish to hike, and also for access to the remote mountain villages in the range. The path occasionally coincides with the track, and at one of the few sections where it joined, we had our first sight of a troop of gelada baboons. They were ideally positioned, as if for a photo shoot, on the edge of a huge precipice on a grassy bank.

I kept a respectable distance but Tal, either fearless, experienced, stupid, downright nosy – or most likely a combination of all of these – lolloped right up to the alpha male on all fours and sat down less than two metres away. Elad and I followed sheepishly. The gelada are the rarest of animals; unique to Ethiopia, they live within the highlands. The males don long, lionesque manes with handsomely tufted tails, and have a unique red opening on their chests bestowing the oft-used sobriquet, 'bleeding heart baboon'. The young ones cavorted with each other in the sunshine while the rest of the troop completely ignored both them and us, preoccupied with the more rewarding task of eating grass.

We skirted the edge of the precipice through long grasses in a northeasterly direction until we reached our first camp of Sankaber. We pitched our tents on some flat grass and used one of the open-air mountain huts to cook up a hot dinner for ourselves, Mercabul and Alemu. The temperature dropped sharply with the sun and we were treated to a glorious glowing sunset between a deep westerly-facing valley. In the morning we brewed some hot, sweet *buna* and got an early start after breakfast. It wasn't long before the path led out over a thin rocky bridge flanked by bushy trees onto a natural platform, overlooking a vastly deep gorge with a graceful waterfall spewing spring waters into the hidden depths across the pass.

It was a baking hot day and we all wore T-shirts wrapped around our heads to protect us from the sun. An oxygen-gulping climb led us up and onto the track that took us around the gorge onto the vast grasslands. Descending a valley, we reached the river feeding the waterfall. Taking off our boots, we dipped our feet in the icy waters and had lunch. Some villagers brought their horses and goats down across the ford, paused to drink, then carried on. They were shortly followed by a troop of geladas who descended the steep valley sides with effortless speed and agility, babies clinging on to their mothers like jockeys at the Derby Stakes run at Epsom Downs.

It felt good to be in the mountains which were undeniably stunning. The travel snob in me however could feel that we were doing nothing more than walking a well-trodden path; especially seeing all the busloads of tourists going past on the track, and this feeling was never really dispelled in this range. We continued up the path that led through a picturesque village of grass huts, nestled in the grassland steppe of pale burnished copper, where some children tried to sell us hats. We eventually reaching our second camp in Gich, situated high up on the plateau. We set our tents and cooked for our little male family.

Tal and Elad were the perfect travelling companions. Both younger than me in their mid-twenties, they had both completed their compulsory military training, and had a delightfully carefree attitude to travel, none of us once bemoaning the inevitable hardships, and indeed, rather revelling in them. Elad had short hair and an excellent physique, with a quiet, straightforward type of personality. Tal had long hair tied back in a knot and was by far the most flamboyant of all of us. Every time we reached camp Elad would insist on doing a grueling regime of push-ups to maintain his upper body strength whilst Tal and I would lie resting in the long grass, jeering and throwing pebbles at him to try and distract him from his work ethic.

At mid-morning the following day, we found ourselves on a high peak with one of the best views of the trek. The vista dropped down and took off into a hazy mirage of sunlit rocky tabletop mountain *ambas*, Ethiopia's impregnable natural fortresses of rock. These wore green cummerbunds of foliage, supported at their bases by the pale-yellow fields of *teff* that grow at lower altitudes. Behind the flattened pinnacles, vast waves of stone and burnished forest meandered like wind-blown sand towards an indiscernable horizon. Immediately to the right a village had terraced a lush plateau flecked with juniper trees, its flowing contours a patchwork of bright green and dull butter, depending on when the farmers had planted their barley.

We were so high up, scattered villages on the terraced plateau could be covered from view with a hand palm. Cloud started to come in and broke behind us against the bulwark of the mountain, adding to the mystery and romanticism of the place. We headed down the long winding path to our third camp at Chennek, the cloud in proper now; turning the chasm on our left into a cold, damp white-out. White-headed eagles circled on the damp air directly at eye level or swooped overhead, their long graceful wings working hard to mitigate the lack of thermals. The sounds from the village below were exaggerated by the natural gramophone of its setting; children playing on the dirt porches of their grass houses sounding as if they were being attacked by bandits, their screams for mercy occasionally punctured by the calls of a baboon.

Just as we arrived at the designated campsite, surrounded by simple buildings to fend off the elements, two graceful Walia ibex were foraging around one of the mountain huts, oblivious to human activity. They had very large, thick-ridged horns curving back from their heads, looking more like mountain spirits than a normal animal. I was tired and had already packed my filming equipment away but vowed to get some good footage of them the next day. Of course, we never saw them again so close. We had no objections to a rest-day, which we spent reading, writing, exploring the area, following monkeys, bemoaning the lack of photogenic ibex, chatting with locals and a group of South American tourists we befriended, and generally watching the world go by. A large gelada male kept stealing *injera* from outside a cookhouse and had to be chased off by children with stones.

Sitting on the damp earth eating *injera* from round stainless-steel trays, Ethiopian men working as guides or mulemen wore blankets or beach towels of unpredictable designs. One had a dark green and light green blanket with large flowers patterned on it around his head like a turban, another a red and pink floral blanket that you would expect to see draped over your grandmother's sofa. Tal had consciously infected us all with a local ditty which he would sing constantly: "*Ababaioush – lem lem!*" (I have a flower – it is green). Joined by groups of children, we'd sing and clap time for what seemed like hours on end.

That evening I unwittingly left Mercabul and Alumu alone with the *arake* bottle and upon returning to the shelter we found them exquisitely inebriated, each in the other's arms, topping up their glasses to the very brim, refilling regularly and drinking apace. They were having an absolute whale of a time, and we heard their giggling voices long into the night as they slept together under a large shared blanket. The trail to Bwahit, which at 4437m is the third highest mountain in Ethiopia, is a pretty straightforward air-gulping 'up', and we reached the summit after a few hours climb the next day, only to be enveloped in a fast-moving cloud again. We hung around for a bit but were getting cold with the lack of movement, so we decided to head down. A few hundred metres or so below the summit

I noticed that the cloud had cleared over the pass to our right, revealing a bright blue sky.

"Come on let's cut across; I have a feeling we will get a view from there," I shouted. Coming up over the brow, we were rewarded with the view of Ras Dashen, at 4550m the highest mountain in the country. It is a great immovable blob of a mountain, a sort of Jabba The Hutt figure, reclining over a parched valley of many folds of baked sun-bleached earth, a lone village of tin-sided huts flashing in the sun like a lost caravan. Its many deep ravines drain rainwater or snowmelt into the Takkazzi and Meshaha rivers. A large cloud loomed just above it, condensing over the squat peak as a feeling of happiness washed over me. It certainly wasn't the most beautiful mountain I had ever seen, if anything it was quite anticlimactic, but there was something about it, it was certainly impressive, I just couldn't quite put my finger on it.

5

THE JUNGLE IN BOLIVIA (2007)

fui por el mundo buscando la vida:
pájaro a pájaro conocí la tierra
I wandered the world in search of life;
bird by bird I've come to know the earth

– Pablo Neruda

I walked along the lagoon at sunset as the mountains turned
a pale blue in the distance and the jungle shone brightly. It
reminded me very strongly of all the Joseph Conrad novels I'd
read towards the end of university, culminating in a messy dis-
sertation trying to compare the anti-colonial sentiments of *Lord
Jim* with the pro-colonial protagonist of Rudyard Kipling's *Kim*.
Noticing large jaguar footprints in the dried mud, I walked
along them on my hands and knees pretending to be a big cat.

Many trunks had roots splaying out about two metres
from the ground, creating spiky wigwams. I passed the time
watching ants carry food to their nests in treetops, fresh pieces
of lime green leaves waggling in the sunlight. On the ground,

more ants pushed up the red earth like lava. The whole place was humming. Accompanied by some Spanish friends, an Argentinian and two English girls, I'd set off for a week's adventure in the Amazon from Rurrenabaque, a small town on the banks of the Beni River famous for its trails that lead to the rainforests and pampas of northern Bolivia.

Our indigenous Bolivian guide, Sandro, had grown up in the jungle completely wild with bare feet and clothes made from tree bark. We also had a local cook called Freddie, a wonderfully flamboyant homosexual. I had finished university that year, and living at my grandparent's house in London, had amassed what was to me a small fortune doing telephone sales for a data company over the summer. I had bought a one-way ticket to South America intending to live there.

On the fifth night we pitched camp next to a lagoon in a hut made of leaves with mosquito nets inside. It belonged to an indigenous man and his shoeless children. I was cutting down bamboo in the jungle for our camp when the man came along the path carrying a rifle. One of his sons trotted behind carrying a large catch of fish. He had killed them with a bow and arrow to save bullets. He gave us one of his fish, which was enough to feed eight of us with rice, and we gave him and his family three bowls of soup in exchange. We sat around the fire while I played the fiddle (which I had insisted on bringing with me) to his astonished children who had swollen bellies from the fermented maize drink *chicha*.

It turned out the man's wife had died, and he was raising the children himself. The Argentinian had packed some simple medicines like paracetamol and antibiotics, which he offered to the native man, in case his children ever got sick. The native man couldn't read, so the labels were useless even though they were written in Spanish. This unknown realm of knowledge created a look of confusion and fear in his eyes that was pitiful to behold. He would never understand how to administer the medicines, making me worry for his young, fragile family. In my youthful idealism I had been expecting to find a kind of utopian way of life in the Amazon – the thought of which had sustained me through this first horrendous job in the city – but my first experience of this harsh reality of this was not what I had expected.

We went deeper into the jungle and camped for two more nights, spending a day exploring virgin forest. There is a tree that looks like a palm but it has bright blue berries called *assai* and to climb it – the fruit is about four storeys up – you tie a t-shirt into a circle and put your feet inside pulling it taught, and it helps you to shimmy up although it is pretty tiring work with the machete swinging from a vine tied to your jeans. The berries when mashed make a very delicious and refreshing drink. We saw wild pigs, monkeys, toucans, parrots and capybaras, which I had never seen before and look like massive guinea pigs, about the size of a large dog. Our camp consisted of a large tarp suspended over a beam and tied to stakes in each corner, a tarp for the floor and then two long beams raised about a metre off the ground to hang our mosquito nets on. We had a fire going all the time.

One incident of note on this first trip: While exploring the virgin forest, Sandro went ahead with a machete hacking out a path for us. One of the English girls wanted to have a go, so Sandro gave her the machete and told us all to stay well back. He later told me he heard a metallic 'Ping!' and knew from experience this was the noise a machete makes when it has hit a tree and someone has let go of the handle. He instinctively swung his face away as the machete sailed through the air slicing his face open from the corner of his mouth up the side of his nose. As blood came gushing out, one of the Spanish girls ripped off her T-shirt and used it to stop the bleeding.

Sandro took one of our water bottles and cut it in half to make a cup and pulled down his fly and pissed into it. He then poured the urine onto the deep cut and the bleeding stopped almost immediately. He led us back to camp, where Freddy and I tended his wound along with some help from a tiny puppy the Argentinian had insisted on bring along. A bit of a nuisance up until now, the obliging animal disinfected Sandro's wound by licking it clean. We all knew if Sandro had not moved his head, he would have been killed, and we would probably all have died in the jungle as we were an hour away from camp and three days from the nearest village. Sandro gets poorly paid by the trekking company and when we were all throwing in for a tip for him and Freddy, I distinctly remember the English girl who had let go of the machete saying of Sandro's tip; "… well we shouldn't all put too much in because then he will have loads!"

After a few days in town, I paid Sandro what I would have paid the trekking company directly in advance to guide me alone for a week in the jungle. I felt that there was more for me out there, and I didn't want to be held back by the tourists, who's behavior I had found questionable at best. He took me to meet his family, who lived on the fringes in a bamboo house with a high thatched grass roof. They were very poor. When I paid him directly, he was able to buy a television for the first time, along with corrugated metal for an extension to the house which I helped him to build using machetes, a hammer and nails.

The toilet, a grass thatched outhouse, had blown down a few weeks before and was now completely infested with ants, so we burned it and put up a new one – getting extremely bitten in the process. By the time we'd finished, the house was almost twice as big. Sandro's three very young daughters sat inside giggling at the television. We met early the next day to buy supplies for our trip: batteries for two torches, a camera for me (which didn't work), a small bag of rice, oil, sugar, salt, coca leaves, alcohol and tobacco. These are all of vital importance in the jungle. We ate empanadas at the market, then took a boat across the river, jumped on two motorcycle taxis and sped off into the wilderness.

The road was a deep red and cut into the lime green jungle like an open vein. The roads in Bolivia are very bad and every time we crossed a deep ford, I was sure the water would suffocate the engines – but it didn't. My driver almost crashed when we hit a big rock, but he was obviously used to it and steadied the bike at the last moment. Dropped off at the side of the road, we headed through long grass towards the mountain range that had been rolling along beside us. We walked for eight hours the first day and were both completely soaked in sweat. The mountains were extremely steep and we often had to scramble up on our hands and feet from rock to rock using vines and roots as ropes.

Sandro stopped and showed me a very poisonous snake that was a light brown colour and impossible to distinguish from the surroundings. He swiftly cut off its head. I was glad he was walking in front. Reaching a small summit and ridge, we hiked along the winding peaks for an hour or so until we came to an opening in the foliage. Beyond the road was the longest, flattest plain I had ever seen, dotted with mossy treetops and threaded with blue ribbon of river. Sandro pointed north and said simply, 'Amazonia'. Scrambling down proved to be harder going than ascending. We found some small bright orange fruit and put them in our packs for later, then took a long drink when we found a stream.

Following its meander, we found a beautiful spot with waterfalls and pools. Slippery rocks made it easy to slide down on your bum, although the higher you went the more leeches there were. After making the usual inspections of our battered skin, we pulled off the ticks and had a good wash. We stopped at a fallen tree and peeled back the bark looking for grubs to use as fishing bait. Our camp was set by a deep lagoon, where we fished using line with a hook pulled in by hand. Sandro caught two silvery whoppers and thought it was hilarious when I dragged out two turtles – which are prohibited to eat. We cooked the fish on the fire with rice and had sugar water for dessert. It felt like the best meal I had ever eaten.

Sandro sneakily produced a half-eaten mosquito net which we hung up and although I slept well, I was tired when I got up. The fish were biting less and less so we packed up and headed down the stream stopping at each good spot. Lagoons would always form because of huge mossy rocks and it seemed that each place was more beautiful than the last. A large bright blue butterfly the size of an outstretched hand had landed on a green rock in the middle of a babbling brook and died. It shone like a gem and I pressed it in one of my books. I caught a good-sized fish and Sandro reeled in one so big it would last us for three days.

We made camp where the river canopy was wide enough to see a decent amount of sky, and watched the sun go down then the stars come out between the overhanging jungle. We slow-cooked the fish in leaves and ate it on plates of bark and a table of leaves. Drinking the bottle of Singani that I had snuck along, distilled from white Muscat of Alexandria grapes, it felt like we were dining like kings. We retired to our leaf house and tried to ignore the heat by sitting in our underpants talking about this and that. Sandro would always light a candle to *Pachamama* [Mother Nature], sprinkling some coca leaves in front of it. He'd light a cigarette from a fresh packet and let it burn down and would pour a drop of alcohol every time he took a sip. Naturally I followed the procedure.

I had been experiencing diarrhea of the most exotic and delightful colours and my tummy was playing up. Sandro made me some tea with tree bark and I slept for an hour and a half. Upon awakening, I felt much better and discovered Sandro had drunk the entire bottle of Singani and was having a wonderful time. He was very entertaining to listen to – although rather hard to understand with coca leaves stuffed in his cheek, a cigarette between his lips and a hefty slur on his Spanish. Sandro is short with curly black hair that covers his ears and a handsome face. He never had any trouble bedding female tourists who passed through. He has a slim, tanned body that masks an unbelievable strength and endurance. Sitting there in his pants, fantastically drunk and swaying with his enormous grin and scorpion eyes, the wound on his face beginning to heal, I felt that I wouldn't want to be in the jungle with anyone else.

Our shopping preparations had not been in vain: coca leaves in the jungle relieve hunger and give you energy when normally you would be completely exhausted. There is something about the jungle that is very draining when you are not accustomed to it. You are constantly hassled by insects and thorns, and you have to constantly be alert to the many dangers. Coca helps keep you sharp. Alcohol is also useful to help you sleep when mixed with water, to disinfect bites and to start fires when everything is soaking. Tobacco seems to be solely for morale although it is good for keeping mosquitoes away for a blessed few minutes. Salt is vital to prevent dehydration because you sweat buckets all the time, and sugar also helps to keep your energy levels up. It is amazing what a difference these simple compounds make at the end of a very long day.

In the morning I got up first and made some sugar tea (we would burn some on a spoon in the fire to add colour) for Sandro who naturally was feeling a little delicate. We washed our clothes in the river and hung them on branches. We had more fish and leftover rice but were horrendously plagued by wasps and flies that drove me to distraction. Sandro had a nap while I either splashed around in the river or went butterfly catching. We found an assai tree, shimmied up and cut down the fruit and took it back to make a drink with dinner.

Sandro woke up in the night and this time it was his stomach playing up. I made him some bark tea and the next day he was completely cured. It is very strong stuff. We listened to howler monkeys, the constant humming of crickets and steady rhythms of the frogs. The pleasant symphony was rudely inter-rupted by a herd of about fifty wild pigs wallowing in a small creek. We went to watch them but they sensed us and the hair went up on their backs and they came towards us so we had to climb a tree and make growling noises until they all wandered off into the undergrowth. The smell emanating from the herd was horrendous.

We planned to go spear fishing, and as I was cleaning my teeth in the river I was very excited. I watched the toothpaste fall down into the water in little explosions and float away over the rocks and I hoped that somewhere along the way a mosquito would somehow get trapped in it and die. We found a very long circular tree that is covered in spines and cut it down to shape bows. The wood on the outside was incredibly tough and it felt like I was clanging my machete against a lamppost as we hacked it down. The middle wood was very soft however, allowing the bow to compress without splitting if you shape the bow so the soft wood faces you. Sandro spent an hour shaping his and mine took three times as long although it was just as good and in fact a little stronger.

Using long serrated arrowheads made from wood, we stalked down the river barefoot from rock to rock. The jungle was completely untouched and glistened in the hot sun. Kingfishers would dart from bank to bank in emerald streaks and toucans and parrots flashed their bright colours between the leaves. Being careful not to allow the fish to see my shadow, I caught one on the tail, but the arrow went harmlessly through the fin and it swam off. Another time I was so close the shaft stunned the fish but as I leapt into the water swinging my machete it came to its senses and was too quick for me.

Sandro had made his arrow too light and it kept glancing upwards when it hit the water and it was hilarious to hear his constant curses. We decided to switch tactics, using a grub found in some bamboo to catch a piranha to use as bait. We threw out our lines and caught four giants in about five minutes. One of the fish had no scales but a soft skin patterned like a shark and long feelers like a catfish and is called *Pintow*. Hooking one on each end of our bows, we carried them back to camp, while some fire ants made my left arm feel like it was in a furnace for half an hour.

Exhaustion was a regular occurrence. I seemed to be able to walk forever but when we stopped my body would sometimes refuse to function normally. The hardest test was tying the leaves to our A-frame every night with twine which is fiddly at the best of times, and when one is tired it is enough to reduce a grown man to tears. It was Sandro's turn to watch me get drunk on some of the rubbing alcohol we'd carried to help heal any injuries. The constant molestation of the jungle was starting to get to me, and I needed the mental escape. Finally, I slept.

Heading towards Tuichi River the following day, I dawdled in the rear singing songs and pretending to be fine. After arriving, we made a raft out of four dead logs lashed together with some small rope we had and then vines. I was hungover but can honestly say that the jungle was wearing me down and my morale was very low at that point. My skin was battered from the constant bites and moisture. The sun was out and shone down on the riverbank so I pulled down my shorts to get the sun's rays on the white and now blotchy red irritated skin on my bottom to try and dry it out. I caught Sandro's scorpion eyes and I knew that he knew that I was beaten in that moment. Just another soft Westerner.

We pushed out into the river and flowed gently down the rapids, paddling when the current became too sluggish. We hit a shallow rock and one of the crossbeams snapped so we pulled into the bank and lashed on a new one. We continued in this manner for a couple of hours until a boat came up behind us and we flagged it down and jumped in with our rucksacks. The boat was made of a huge hollowed log, thirty feet long, with wooden sides added on to make a prow and a tarp roof. One of Sandro's friends was sitting up front with his wife and child and he had on a red cap and aviator sunglasses. His young son was strumming a guitar. As we cruised between sandy beaches leading to green mountains, the weather closed in and it rained very heavily.

As we arrived back to Rurrenabaque, we jumped out into the wet sand in our sandals, and took two motorcycle taxis to Sandro's house. We had banana cake and coffee for dinner. I bought some Coca-Cola which seemed like an unbelievable luxury. His girls were watching 'The Young Indiana Jones' dubbed in Spanish. I slept on comfy blankets covering the mud floor, listening to the crickets still humming outside and felt relieved to be away from the insects. The next day I discovered Sandro's wife was sick and had been having severe stomach pains for weeks. Yet Sandro had used the money I had given him to extend his house and buy a television rather than help her receive medical attention. The painful memory of the motherless family we had encountered in the jungle loomed large in my mind.

But I couldn't effectively confront him about it, as there was something so careless in his attitude whereby my shock and anger just seemed to melt away. Sandro was a wild man who lived by the laws of nature but this seemed to me either needlessly cruel at worst, or woefully uneducated at best. I just couldn't understand what was motivating his apathy. Maybe the lure of a television was just too great to withstand. Fortunately, a tourist I knew was heading to the capital city, La Paz, the next day and agreed to take her to a hospital and pay for her treatment. I never found out what happened to her and I lost contact with Sandro as he never replied to my emails.

In many ways this trip marked a significant change in me, as I had often mentally shunned modern civilization in favour of an idealistic return to ancient ways of living in nature. But I had never truly appreciated just how hard and unforgiving these can be, or how a lack of the most basic of education can so easily lead to needlessly devastating consequences.

6

ETHIOPIA: THE AFAR –
AKA MY DANAKIL DEPRESSION (2015)

Better to die than to live without killing.

– Afar adage

The semi-nomadic Afar tribe, who reside in the northeastern deserts of Ethiopia on the Eritrean border, were for centuries feared for their ferocious nature and warlike culture. Legendary British explorer Sir Wilfred Patrick Thesiger, the son of a diplomat based in Addis Ababa, declared in his memoirs that the most dangerous journeys of his life were those among Ethiopia's Afar tribe, in the region of the same name – and this after having lain starving to death on a sand dune for three days in Saudi Arabia's *Rub' al Khali* [Empty Quarter] before his Bedu companions brought him desperately needed supplies.

In the past, the Afar had a reputation for cutting off an enemy's testicles as trophies and presenting them to brides on their wedding day as a sign of their bravery. Thesiger, in 1953 saw at least one young Afar man flushed from the exertion of slaughtering and mutilating four victims in a single day, described him as, "the equivalent of a nice, rather self-conscious Etonian who had just won his school colours for cricket". In the 10th century, the Afar came into contact with the Arabs and converted to a form of Islam, merging it with their old indigenous beliefs. To this day, they continue to worship a dominant sky-god. Much of their once proud culture is said to have now been lost however.

The Danakil Depression, in the northern part of the Afar region, is one of the hottest places on earth in terms of year-round average temperatures. In terms of altitude, it's one of the lowest points, registering 116m below sea level at its nadir. As if this wasn't enough, it is also one of the most tectonically active areas in the world resulting from the presence of three tectonic plates causing several lava crater lakes to bubble up from the earth's core. It is referred to as *the cradle of the humanoids* after the famous 'Lucy' *Australopithecus* fossil was discovered here in 1974, dated to be 3.2 million years old.

Along with Tal and Elad, my trusted Israeli companions from the Simien Mountains, we somewhat reluctantly joined a tour group to scope out the region, as we didn't particularly feel like going this one alone. At the time Ethiopia was still in its decades-long conflict with the country of Eritrea to the north, with peace only finally being achieved in 2018. As the Afar region borders Eritrea, flare-ups of fighting in this area were not uncommon. But if it makes money it makes sense: tourists want to see this unique area and so local tour companies have been happy to meet this demand. The British Government were advising against travel to the region at the time, but that had never stopped me before, and Tal and Elad were equally sanguine.

We set off from the town of Mekele in a convoy of seven Toyota Land Cruisers, passing farmsteads and rocky scrub-covered foothills which soon gave way to desolate, enclosed plains. A blue sky was interspersed with clouds and the shadows of these moved across the sandy mountains encircling the flat-lands. It was Christmas Day and the air was starting to get hot. We drove up from one plain then down into another, then up again into green-freckled mountains. The freckles grew into strange cactus-trees with circular clumps of foot-long tendrils. Everything was painted in pastel colours, leading from far-off shades of emerald and silver glinting on the high peaks.

Children played by the roadsides of the tiny towns. A woman with piercing green eyes stood on a hillside, a red and black chequered shamma draped around her head and body, looking like a model in a photo shoot. Villagers carrying yellow plastic containers collected water from thin streams meander-ing through wide river plains. One woman had a baby strapped to her back in a sheet of black cotton flecked with green. Her companion wore a black headscarf with a silvery latticework grate on her forehead resembling a tiny portcullis. Despite the extreme sparseness, filth and drabness of these mountain villages, both women were elegant and carried themselves with dignity.

British writer Elizabeth Laird spent many years travelling around Ethiopia in collaboration with the British Council, collecting folk stories from all of the different regions, and pub-lishing her experiences in *The Lure of the Honey Bird*. Although taken from stories collected in the Somali region (not to be confused with the separate country of Somalia) directly to the south of the Afar region, the following resonated very strongly with me as I looked at the young Afari girls, considering the life in store for them, and the suffering of young women in the country as a whole.

"The one [story] I shall never forget, one of the most remarkable I ever heard in Ethiopia, expresses in the most poignant way the terror of a girl-child, barely in her teens, facing her unknown bridegroom on her wedding night. She will have already suffered a brutal and unhygienic circumcision, her labia excised with a dirty knife or piece of broken glass, and her vagina may have been crudely stitched, leaving only a small hole for the passage of menstrual blood. It will be slashed open with her new husband's knife before he penetrates her. Looking ahead, she will soon have to face the terror of giving birth, which many young brides are too small to survive. This story … is truly a woman's story."

The men wore their shammas as long skirts wrapped around their waists, occasionally tied up at the front at knee-level to allow greater flexibility of movement. I often saw them play fighting or just plain fighting with one another. The 4x4s continued on and as the hours rolled past the plains grew larger and termite hills and lone camels began to appear. Children shepherded flocks of goats alone in the wilderness. Dwellings were made from sacking, rock, branches, or simply pulled together from anything else that could be salvaged including the tin roofing from a now derelict health center and car tyres.

The plain gave a last gasp of undulation then gave out to the dead flat pan of the depression. More desperate looking hamlets clung to the new road. I found it hard to imagine the life of the people living here. One young man was standing outside a particularly bleak construction holding an old Nokia-style mobile phone in his hand. Around him was a complete desolation of black lava rock. I wondered what he was texting. The vehicles finally stopped and our tour group of about twelve people all got out and stretched. A group of middle-aged Japanese tourists were camped alongside a large salt lake, where huge piles of salt were heaped all around the shores as far as the eye could see.

It was not what you would call beautiful. The local town was little more than a propped-up shithole littered with trash. It felt strange to be in such a barren, desolate place and to be surrounded by tourists. I didn't really know what I was doing there. After such a great trip in the Simien Mountains, myself, Tal & Elad just felt we were now on a conveyor belt of people being moved around to make money, which indeed we were. After floating on the surface of the salt water in the sunset, we rinsed off in the baking hot natural pool of a freshwater spring. Someone had left their AK47 lying around.

We slept in the open in a compound on the edge of town on goat hide-latticed beds. We built a huge fire and danced around it long into the night, drinking ouzo with the tour guides. Some locals came for the food and drink but just sat on their haunches around a fire and no one really seemed to connect, but it was Christmas after all so we made the best of it. During the night, I realized I was getting mauled by bedbugs hidden in my mattress, which I subsequently hurled onto the floor, choosing to sleep on the bare hide thongs instead. Then it started to rain, so I dragged my bed in underneath a tin shack.

"It never rains here," said one of the guides the next morning.

We drove off-road across a dusty plain at the foot of a large extinct volcano. The going became more difficult when we hit a lava rock field and we slowed to a crawl over the track in the unforgiving landscape. The rock was extremely sharp, and I was amazed we didn't blow a tyre. After a long day we arrived at the Ethiopian military outpost guarding the base camp, for our ascent to the active volcano of Etra Ale.

We were very close to the Eritrean border. To the bemusement of my driving companions I had managed to consume a couple of hundred pages of modern Ethiopian history during even the bumpiest sections of the journey. I had lost count of the number of invasions and counter-invasions over the centuries between Ethiopia and her northeastern neighbour, the latter now keeping her land-locked from the important trade links of the Red Sea. Relations continue to be strained and it is still an unstable region.

News of skirmishes and arrests are restricted from press publication by the government. But I discovered some German tourists were murdered here a few years back for no particular reason. Despite this, I was happy to take my chances along with everyone else. The military outpost was comprised of sturdy stone huts populated by well-equipped soldiers. Camels lounged on the ground with forked sticks like dowsing rods down their sides for baggage or two sets of criss-crossed poles for passengers. One Indian family with three young children opted to ride instead of doing the three-hour hike, the children quite obviously having the time of their lives.

It was strange to see such a young family in this place. I wondered if they understood the geopolitics in the region, or if they were just blindly following their guide assuming that if there was any danger they would have been informed, or if they knew and they just didn't care. Africa is Africa after all; there is nearly always some sort of unrest going on in one form or another, but it is important to understand the severity, as it can escalate extremely quickly. Of course, this is also part of the appeal, the wildness of the continent Paul Theroux calls 'The Dark Star' always keeping you on your toes, and the blood pumping through your veins. My friend Dom once commented to me that "the best thing about Africa is that you can't think more than a day ahead." And indeed, this can be a blessing – but only up to a point.

We set out after sunset to avoid the heat, a moderate 35°C (temperatures can reach up to 50°C in the summer) due to cloud cover. A full moon lit the way of our track over the lava field as the volcano came into view, a scarlet glow emanating from the top, reflected on the underside of the dark cloud. Upon reaching the summit we encountered more stone, thatched huts and camels reclining on folded legs, tied at the knee, chewing the cud. Between two of the huts the flat summit dropped thirty metres down some steep rocky steps to violent folds of dark black stone and clinker. A peak jutted upwards in a 45-degree incline ending in a sheer vertical drop, exactly as I had imagined the setting of the *orc* tower when reading JRR Tolkien's *The Lord of the Rings*. And there, a few hundred metres away across the stone field, we could see the rim of the huge lava lake smoking gently, a mist of angry red hovering above it.

It started to rain. "It never rains here," said another guide.

We stood facing the lava pit, with cold, wet backs, then turned around so our clothes could dry off instantly in the scalding heat, then repeated the process. "So," I heard someone say, mirroring exactly my own thoughts, "this is how the world was formed." It was a humbling experience to see solid rock reduced to a malleable liquid, solidifying momentarily in a thin skin upon contact with the cold night air, then cracked apart, revealing its shining underbelly, pulled down again into the depths of the perfectly circular lake.

The rain hissed as it evaporated. The lava bubbled up on the left side of the lake with a palpable force, hitting the lee of the overhanging lake's crust, spewing the walls and air with tiny missiles. The lava would then drift along to the right side where it was pulled back down into the depths once more if not caught in one of the eruptions in the middle. The molten rock shone a bright amber and blood-red, as hypnotic as the innermost embers of a log fire. A furry, lichen-like moss grew on the banks of the crater. The skin on my face burned.

We stayed for a couple of hours then headed back to our huts in the rain. The mattresses brought up by the camels were now all sodden, although I had had no intention of using them anyway. Joined by a Finnish contingent of tourists we had befriended, we sat in a circle chatting for a while. Our sleeping bags were still dry, and we got a few hours' sleep on the earthen ground.

During an uneventful descent through a bleak sunrise, we encountered the middle-aged Japanese posse armed with sunhats and walking poles, starting to climb just as the day was heating up. Although ill-informed, I had to respect their pluck. We embarked on the daylong journey out to the salt flats, arriving at another army base in the evening where we slept outside on wicker beds. The only highlight of the drive was a huge eight-foot wild ostrich who came belting across the track in front of us, running from nowhere to nowhere, its huge legs working like mechanical pistons kicking up dust and gravel. A strange creature in a strange place, a desolate and hostile land.

In the morning, we drove down to the salt flats past the long camel trains. Literally hundreds of them marched out in single file into nowhere, the glare of the sun encircling their dark moving silhouettes in the distance. It was as if they were marching back into time itself. Our Land Cruisers rolled through the salty shallows creating small ripples of golden sunlight. We reached an island and walked towards natural sulphur formations of bubbling, smoking green and yellow pools with an abandoned rusting Italian sulfurworks in the distance.

I was surprised at the squealing exclamations of many of the tourists. Even Tal and Elad seemed kind of interested. The eggy fumes made me gag and retch and I retired to a rock outcrop alone overlooking the wasteland to sulk, just waiting to get the bloody thing over with. But I had one final leg to go. Salt blocks have been traded and used as currency in Ethiopia and the surrounding regions for a millennium. The Afar dig and shape the salt from the flats of the Danakil Depression, load them on to their huge camel trains and transport them to the interior, where they are loaded onto donkeys for the higher altitudes. The further a block is transported from the Depression the higher its value. On average, a block of salt is worth 45 Birr (just over two Dollars US).

Afari cutters receive four Birr per block shaped, non-Afari cutters three Birr. This pay doesn't include the two-week round trip needed to transport the blocks to buyers. Temperatures can top 50°C in the summer, making working conditions deplorable. The seven Land Cruisers pulled up to where a hundred or so workers were hacking salt from the baking ground. Tourists jumped out, shoving their cameras in the workers' faces to take pictures. I felt awkward and mildly disgusted. One sharp-witted cutter with wraparound sunglasses remarked to one particularly portly German in a khaki waistcoat: "I live on the moon."

I went back to my vehicle and sat in the shade of the engine with one of the Finnish contingent, who was having a similar reaction to the situation. An overwhelming number of tourists say that visiting the Danakil Depression is by far and away the highlight of their trip to Ethiopia, some even their lives. I could not have felt more strongly towards the opposite.

7

CAIRO (2015)

"Welcome Mr. Sam. Although check-in time is at two o'clock, we will have your room ready for you in a few minutes. I have booked you into a suite. It is no problem." I sat in a comfy lobby chair on a shiny marble floor that rolled on forever watching a woman smoke a cigarette while her two male companions dozed on couches, before a bellhop led me up to my room. Shower. Coffee. Phone rings.

"Mr. Waleed is here for you, Mr. Sam."

"Very good. I'm coming down."

I was determined to get in some sight-seeing before work began. We pulled out of the driveway in my pre-arranged driver Waleed's oversized KIA that had taken a considerable beating around the front bumper and flanks, although it remained in good condition on the inside. "I'll always prefer it this way around," Bashar later commented with his usual accuracy when I described it to him. We arrived at Giza and I persuaded Waleed to come with me as 'guide' so I would take less flak from the hawkers. We parked up and walked past lightweight horses pulling lightweight wooden carts for tourists filled with bright bundles of fresh long green grass on the seats. The street smelled like shit and they treated the horses abominably.

I bought our tickets and we entered through the gate. I was looking at the Sphinx and the pyramids and felt like I had somehow cheated by getting here so easily. The day before, I had been watching raindrops tap against the office windows of Finsbury Square as I printed off meeting locations on Google Maps and finished off PowerPoint slides. It was like I had rushed a kiss. It was too soon. I hadn't built up to this. I still felt full up after overeating an expenses-paid airport dinner followed by an airline dinner, just because I could.

Waleed took a photo of me by the Sphinx. A fly had flown into the top right-hand corner of the photo leaving a fuzzy grey fly-sized smudge. I also felt emotionally bloated and flabby; faced with such a timeless monument as this, it emphasized how much crap I was carrying around in my head. Once we were closer to the pyramids and beyond the hawkers, I started to lose my self-consciousness. The place was practically deserted. Before the revolution, 30,000 tourists visited here every day. I saw less than 30.

Waleed had earlier admitted that although born and raised in Giza, he had never entered the area and walked around the pyramids. I was less surprised at this than I could have been. A young man called Islam disarmed me with his impeccable English and a genuine sense of humour. Now I had a second 'guide'. Waleed's knowledge of the pyramids was less than mine, which was zero, so I justified to myself that it was useful to have someone around who had at least a basic grasp of the facts. Islam went through the names of the pyramids with

Waleed nodding furiously and with grave interest at this revelation, until, unable to contain his enthusiasm any longer, he again admitted to Islam in Arabic that he had never been to the pyramids before.

"Waleed says he has never been to the pyramids before even though he is born here."

"Yes" I replied, "He is the best guide in Egypt."

We all laughed. The great pyramid of Khufu rises from the baked plains like an angry god, swatting away generations of empires like flies from his jagged bulwarks. Khafre, still capped with two-foot-thick limestone casing blocks at the tip, is more feminine and sits to the south west of Khufu on slightly higher ground. Menkaura, the third and smallest of the pyramids, further along again on the southwest bearing, has the least erosion on the finely carved granite stones of her now exposed underbelly, ever so slightly rounded at the edges like the indentations of a tortoise shell.

In Greek: Cheops, Chephren and Mycerinus; once their outer-casings of fine white polished limestone would have emblazoned them in shining fire from the god of the midday sun. We were standing in the ruins of a temple structure with lumps of stone strewn out into the desert.

"Look at this," said Islam as he picked up and broke in half a thin slither of lime. The bright white crystals glistened in the overbearing light and heat of the sunshine. "Imagine the whole pyramid shining like this. They took it down to build houses with. Once there was a big earthquake [AD 1300] and it loosened the stones. You've seen Muhammad Ali Mosque?"

"Yes!?" said Waleed.

"They used this stone to build that mosque."

"No!" Waleed was mortified. It's the biggest mosque in Cairo.

We met two government officials astride camels on the south side of Khafre. They had khaki shirts, bushy moustaches, brown skin and white teeth. Their legs were crossed neatly around the polished wood of the saddle grips. One wore a beret. They were there to regulate the non-existent tourists. "Fuck this I'm going home," said one in Arabic, but they just sloped off a few yards away from us and carried on chatting under the blazing sun.

We climbed over some rocks to the temple ruins of Menkaura and were joined by a bolshie policeman. His pistol was delicately perched in its holster right at the front of his respectable paunch, so it preceded him everywhere he went. It was like he had found the perfect angle for a quick draw, although he was only interested in hassling Waleed and waiting for me to pay Islam so he could get a cut. Due east the plain fell away down to where they bury the Mussulmen of Giza and the terracotta sprawl of Cairo. To the south the pale dunes opened up to the horizon and I instinctively walked out into them but had to turn back when the policeman started yelling at me.

My trip to Cairo then fell into the rather dull, predictable rhythm of work. I had business meetings during the daytime and in the evenings would take a swim in one of the hotel's tree-lined pools or lift weights in the gym. My Jordanian colleague and superior Bashar, who ran the Middle East office, joined me for two days from Dubai. What we thought was going to be a straight-forward meeting with the Ministry of Petroleum turned into myself giving a two-hour presentation to 50 attendees of their affiliate companies in their auditorium complete with plastic flowers and cans of disgusting non-alcoholic malt drink. I did the presentation in English with Bashar apologizing in Arabic and stalling for time whenever their internet connection went down, which I needed to demonstrate financial products.

We had two other meetings that day with two new prospects, one an investment bank literally at the farthest point of the city from us. At the end of it all, we were completely exhausted. Slumped in our hotel bar, we ate peanuts and drank beer, while listening to a gangly girl with the voice of an angel but terrible song choices. Her musical accomplice was a sweaty fat man who insisted on singing all his songs in a different language – first Arabic, then Italian, then French, whilst constantly gyrating with little salsa dance steps.

In the morning we had a meeting with an investment fund in plush new offices on the bank of the Nile that smelt of fresh paint. We were early and sat in the lobby of the Four Seasons next door drinking coffee and looking at the well put together women having lunch. I pulled out and read a few pages from a slim copy of Ranulph Fiennes' memoirs of fighting for the Sultan of Oman in Dhofar in the 1970s.

"This is much more like it," noted Bashar to nobody in particular.

"What sitting in a hotel lobby? I would have thought you'd be sick of hotel lobbies."

"No. The rest of this city is a dump."

"How can you say that? This city has got soul. I like it. It's frenetic. The people are friendly," I said looking at a busty woman with enough lip-gloss on to lubricate a car factory.

"No way. Give me Dubai anytime. Its civilized and it's tidy."

"You call Dubai civilized?"

"Well no, I guess not. But it *is* tidy."

"Well. One out of two ain't bad."

"Ha. Come on let's go."

We went up to the meeting with a very senior player in the country's energy sector. His office window was bathed in golden sunlight from the flowing waters of the river outside. Bashar conducted the meeting solely in Arabic while I sat there looking affable and stupid. I had been doing these kinds of business trips for six years. Three international financial media jobs in London, Dubai and London again had afforded me the means to see world, but were starting to take their toll. It was still exciting – travel is always exciting – but as I sat there, I somehow felt different; Egypt had so much richness and depth, and in comparison, I just felt completely empty inside my expensive suit.

My parents had come out to Egypt in the 80s for a holiday, visiting their friends Flavio and Judith who were still now based in Cairo. I had emailed them before coming out and they invited me for dinner at their apartment one evening. An event quickly cropped up in our conversation that I had always remembered, but not known they had also been a part of: On a hill-walking trip in England when I was seven or eight years old, my dad's friend John Palmer had used the tyre of Flavio and Judith's white Citroen to tie the shoelaces of his leather walking boots as we prepared to set off. It was one of the old Citroens with engine-powered suspension, so that when Flavio turned off the ignition the back of the car sank down trapping John's foot under the wheel hub.

We were all crying with laughter at the time (and in the re-telling), especially Flavio who kept dropping the keys and wiping away the tears in his eyes as he tried to re-start the engine while John howled and flailed his arms half in mock, half in genuine agony. Although this was just a funny memory, the associations I had with it were of a stronger nature; good friends and their families going out into the countryside, enjoying each other's company, having wholesome fun. It seemed worlds away from the direction my life was heading, and I felt ashamed.

"The Copts are as batty as the Muslims," observed Judith over starters of mozzarella, tomato and avocado. "They consider themselves – and I suppose they are really – the only direct descendants of the original Egyptians. When the Arabs invaded, they made everyone swear allegiance to Islam and those who didn't convert, they forced to pay a tax. The Copts being highly Orthodox Christians (they have their own Pope here by the way) wouldn't renounce their faith so paid the tax and didn't mingle as much with the Arabs."

"I always thought the original Egyptians were Nubians from Sudan, how could they possibly be Christians?" I asked, delighted to find a source of historical information. "Well yes that's exactly right, there was a Nubian Dynasty. But the Pharaoh's time ended when the Romans came and you had all that going on between Anthony and Cleopatra. She actually had a son by Caesar, Ptolemy Caesarion (who she also used to sleep with by the way), and was destined to rule Egypt until Octavian was victorious and had Caesarion murdered and the rest killed themselves as you'll know if you've read your Shakespeare. Christianity then spread from the Roman Empire. They were absolute animals and smashed the place up dreadfully. Will you have some bread?"

This conversation had been sparked by my admiring an ornate Coptic silver candlestick holder with its four pearly candles dripping wax onto the middle of the tablecloth. Its light danced in a huge aged Rococo mirror on the wall, painted in now flaking gold, that looked as romantic, glamorous and as run down as the city itself. Judith sat opposite me with Flavio on my right at the end of the long dining table. Their large apartment was beautifully decorated, and I especially admired four very large Turkish blue and white ceramic pots on a dark wooden chest. Naturally the conversation drifted to politics.

"What we have seen is a revolution followed by a counter revolution. What really happened is that when the people stood up to Mubarak something happened that they didn't really intend to happen. The Muslim Brotherhood slipped into power and filled the vacuum when this had never really been the plan in the lead up to the revolution for most people," explained Flavio.

"The Egyptians are deeply religious people. They don't go around saying 'Salaam Alleikum' all day like in the Gulf, but at heart, they are deeply religious. Under the Brotherhood they didn't like the oppressiveness. I certainly didn't like it but you know I thought it was good for the country; I thought that as they had democratically elected a party that actually they didn't really like, they could then democratically elect a party that they did like. And the fundamentalists couldn't complain anymore because they were in power and now had the spotlight on them for a change to actually benefit the country. It was starting to work!"

I poured Flavio another glass of red and he continued.

"Thank you. But then of course it didn't work with the

counter-revolution and now with Sisi in power in what is termed a popular coup.."

"You mean a military coup!" I asked, surprised.

"Well yes, but I certainly wouldn't go around saying that if I were you. Sisi's grip is too tight. He is a military man, he was Minister of Defence under Morsi, and the military has control."

"The petrol queues under Morsi were terrible," added Judith, "but now they have removed the petrol subsidy and the price has gone up 40%. And it is very corrupt. He recently announced that the military doesn't have to pay tax. The military own gas stations, retail outlets and many other businesses as well and now they don't have to pay a penny. Things are calmer now on the streets but there is a lot of resentment underneath it all."

Most of the evening went on like this and I have forgotten most of what we talked about. I drank it in like a river. The deep interest in culture and history, in such a sharp comparison with my daily life of work and routine in London. The problem with the rat race, is that even if you win (which most don't), you are still a rat. I could feel a great sea change coming on. When it was just myself with my driver Waleed, I would alternatively practice my outrageously bad Arabic on him (literally a sitting target), or just stare out of the window at the heat-haze in silence, especially when the desert opened up on the outskirts. I could feel the pull of it. Atop the hazy glow of the setting sun the sky leapt forward with tangible brightness, pierced only by slender minarets as we came back into the city.

Towers of brick rose up to eight storeys high, balanced on floors of thin concrete mixed with too much sand, the profile of their concrete stairs zigzagging up their outsides like the borders of a simple rug. Rivers of bright green crops flowed through vacant plots occasionally leading to a plain of hovels and palm trees. Piles of rubbish lined almost every street, the carcass of a dead horse stiffening in rigor mortis. Young men hawked bundles of drooping coriander between backed-up cars on the highway whilst their families squatted in makeshift homes in the cemeteries. At least half the buildings unfinished and uninhabited, they crowded around the crumbling ruins of grand dilapidated mansions of European architecture, relics of Cairo's belle époque.

I passed through a barbed-wire barricade and waddled down the road leading to the Egyptian Museum on my last day. Bedford police troop trucks flanked either side with unarmed men in black uniforms sitting around. These ended abruptly and were replaced by 12 six-wheeler desert armoured cars complete with mounted cannon, smoke/tear gas launchers, steel pyramid roofs and inch-thick turret protection plates shielding the vitals of a very hot-looking gunner under an oversized desert-camo helmet. The rosy pink Museum is as an obvious target, but this is also a good roll-out point for Tahir Square, which I recognized from the BBC coverage of the Arab Spring, 50 yards down the street, should a crowd start to form for any reason.

Next door and separating the museum from the banks of the Nile loomed the still burnt-out and gutted shell of Mubarak's huge 12-story National Party headquarters. I bought a ticket and looked at shoots of water spreading out like leaves of a palm tree from the fountain in the museum gardens. In the museum I had stood for a very long time in front of a statue of a black Pharaoh. His features were Negroid and handsome, carved in black stone. The statue was quite badly damaged in places but not enough to deter from the vitality that emanated from every line drawn by the sculptors. I wondered how much vitality still remained in me, and I quit my job shortly after returning to London.

8

ETHIOPIA: THE GHERALTA MOUNTAINS (2016)

The Gheralta Mountain chain, deep within the northern high plateaux of the Tigray region, is highly picturesque. I sat on a high rock hill in the garden of a lodge taking in the big-sky view of a sunset over the cartoon cardboard cut-out shapes of the mountain silhouettes. It was market day and the huge plain in front of me thronged with people and their newly acquired livestock, walking back to their homes.

In the middle of the 4th Century AD, Saint Frumentius brought Christianity to the Axumite Kingdom in what is now the Northern Ethiopian Tigray region. A Syro-Phoenician Greek, he was captured with his brother as a boy, becoming a slave to the King of Axum. Upon obtaining their freedom, the brothers educated the King's heir in the teachings of Christianity, and Frumentius was later appointed as the first Bishop in Axum by the Coptic Orthodox Church of Alexandria, whose Pope then also oversaw the Christians of Syria.

According to local tradition, the churches in the Gheralta Mountains were constructed in the 4th Century by the first Christian kings of Ethiopia, Abraha and Atsbeha, although it is more likely that many are 6th Century constructions, from the time when monasticism was spreading throughout the region. Many of the hermitage caves were expanded to become the enormous edifices that can now be admired flickering in candlelight amid the murmurs of the cream-shawled faithful. The churches have been hewn directly out of the mountainsides by hand, only their slim rock pillars left in place to prevent collapse.

They are found in high, remote places to fend off would-be attackers although this has not always saved them from destruction. In the 10th Century, the Jewish Queen Yodit (Judith) tried to eradicate Christianity by burning many of the churches and their valuable Christian works. An invasion led by Ahmed ibn Ibrahim al-Ghazi 'the Conqueror', a Somali general in the 16th Century, also destroyed many treasures and signs of the destruction can still be seen in many of the churches today. After asking around it wasn't long before I met with Gebre, a youthful local mountain guide of slight build. Always quick to smile, he had quickly risen to the top of the local guiding association, due to his natural intelligence, affability, organizational skills and command of English.

He knew his worth, so I doubt I would have hired him for this first trip as I was desperately trying to keep my expenses down, but he was already employed guiding another group at this time. I hired a Tigrinya boy instead called Bennie (not his real name) as a guide and translator, as he knew the area well, but was cheap due to his inexperience. A smile creased the twin scars on either side of his eyes, a common ritualistic sign of Christianity here, as well as a small cross either scarred or tattooed in the middle of the forehead. A policeman had joined us for the ride, and I had complimented him on his beautifully patterned green and red silky shamma, which he wore loosely in a loop around his neck.

He told me it was of the very best quality made by the Afar people in the east. This was met with enthusiastic confirmation by both the driver and Bennie, who explained that it cost upwards of 800 Birr [40 Dollars US] – an impressive sum. The policeman unwrapped it from his neck and splayed the material out lovingly for me to inspect. There was a round sticker in one of the corners that we all read at the same time: 'Made in China.' We all fell about laughing as the minivan bumped along the sandy track, although I chose not to delve into the more negative connotations of this microcosm of the modern world.

The minivan dropped us off outside St. Gabriel's church, a beautiful freestanding structure with whitewashed walls holding three equidistant domed windows on each side. A green slanted roof led up to a second section of squat roofing with a stubby tower painted blue with two tiny red windows. On top of this, three bulbous metal rods held beautifully ornate symmetrical crosses. This and many of the other church buildings, which are often similar in design, reminded me of Tibetan architecture. I have occasionally heard Ethiopia referred to as 'The Tibet of Africa', which I do not think is an outlandish statement. Intrepid Irish explorer and travel writer Dervla Murphy notes in the prologue of her wonderful account *In Ethiopia with a Mule,* first published in 1968, that:

"There is a certain similarity between the developments of Ethiopian Christianity and Tibetan Buddhism. In both cases, when alien religions were brought to isolated countries the new teachings soon became diluted with ancient animist superstitions; and so these cuttings from two great world religions grew on their high plateaux into exotic plants, hardly recognizable as offshoots of their parent faiths."

Our trek began with a scramble up a terraced mountainside and occasional stretches of winding pathway. Once on the top, the views were instantaneously fantastic. We trotted along the ridge of sloping lava rock, alternatively looking down to an acacia-dotted plain and majestic sepia paint stroke lines of rolling foothills. After a small descent we came around a smooth bend in the track over bright purple rock. I remember thinking I had never seen a bright purple rock before. We ascended to our first rock church through the gateway of the priests' dwelling. The Tigrayans, in their arid, rocky plateaux, mainly live in dry-stone buildings compared to the rest of the country who, benefiting from lusher pasturelands, use wood and dung to construct their homes.

I stepped through the roofed archway of the outer wall, where a large iron bell hung from a sturdy beam. As I rounded the corner, I came across six women and an elderly priest standing at the entrance to a doorway cut into the cliff, where a thick curtain allowed the sound of chanting and prayers to emanate from the gloomy interior. This was the rock-hewn church of Yohannis Maqudi.

The women all wore cream shammas and had beautifully

braided hair; thin and tightly woven in different angular patterns along the front section of their heads, their long wavy afro curls then either flying out at the back in large waves or in carefully arranged linear folds and designs. Several wore a single large silver-coloured earring high up on their left ear, hanging in an upturned crescent.

One of the women gestured to me to take off my boots. I did so and went and sat in a small hollowed-out cave next to the priest. The priest wore a cream turban and held his horse-hair fly-whip in a relaxed manor, the symbol of his vocation. Everyone had bare feet, but his feet were so black, they became a different colour within the blackness. I remember thinking this is what the black of a black hole in space must look like. I was strangely fascinated by them. He had a kind face and sang in a soft melodious voice. At one point everyone got down on their knees and elbows on the sandy ground to pray. I did the same and it felt good.

After some sign language it was conveyed to me that I could enter the church if I paid the now regulated donation. The price of which had to be set as many priests were getting carried away with overcharging foreigners to enter the churches. I was led through a dark curving passage, a rudimentary cross chiselled onto the ceiling. This in turn led into the main church up over a second rock-hewn doorway bolstered with thick wooden beams. Inside there were many women and men, all dressed in cream shammas. A priest was intoning prayers while another held a very large latticed brass cross.

The frescos painted onto the hand-chiselled walls were from another time, another world. Warrior saints, the twelve apostles, and Fasilides (Emperor of Ethiopia 1632 – 1667) were all speaking to me through speech bubbles written in Ge'ez, the ancient language of the Ethiopian Christian Church. Their eyes all flashed menacingly. The priests continued to chant, with the congregation occasionally murmuring a response. After mass, the women all filed out through the door I had entered and sat outside under the shade of the acacia. The men all left by the other door and walked to the priest's quarters where they sat with me on earthen benches around a sunken floor. We drank *talla*, a millet-based beer, and ate spongy *injera* with only a chili sauce as everyone was fasting for *Genna*, the Ethiopian Christmas taking place in a week or so.

The segregated all-male atmosphere, though jarring strongly with my Western associations of a Christian community, was extremely welcoming and hospitable; the priests showing a genuine curiosity in me and making sure I wanted for nothing. I suppose some elements of the culture from the neighbouring Islamic Middle East have permeated the Ethiopian form of Christianity to a certain degree. The children silently served their elders with marked deference. The size of my pack was the main topic of conversation, with the priests joking that only a donkey would carry a load like that. After the hearty meal and numerous cups of *talla* later, we shouldered our packs and left the compound. One priest followed us out, loudly demonstrating that I should give him money because he had used the keys to open the church.

There is a strange contradiction in many of the people here, and indeed the whole country, which I had been unable to consciously articulate until coming across another insightful passage of Dervla Murphy's: "One of the strangest paradoxes of highland life is the extraordinary assurance and dignity – of a particular quality not found at all levels in European societies – which distinguishes so many of the peasants. Even in such a remote region as this, and when confronted with such a disquieting phenomenon as myself, their innate courtesy rarely fails them. Yet in many ways they are ignorant, treacherous and cruel to a degree – which has led some foreigners to dismiss their more attractive aspect as a form of deceit, or at best a meaningless routine of etiquette. But to me the two aspects, however contradictory, seem equally genuine."

We came down through a lush eucalyptus grove, over a dry sandy riverbed then up the other side on a path cleft through steep earthy orange embankments. A small freestanding church was nestled into the side of the cliff, its tin roof and cross painted in pleasing bright colours. A bird darted across the valley with oily black feathers and bright auburn wing tips. As we came to the top of a small hill, the dry-stone wall-lined fields of an idyllic valley opened out before us. Young girls playing next to a huge pile of *teff* were screaming their heads off as I slowly walked down the track. "*Faranji*! [foreigner!] Hello!" they repeatedly cried.

The valley was a patchwork of perfectly levelled fields dotted with acacia, olive and eucalyptus. Cacti ran in thick groves, used as a natural fencing around properties. A peach sunset warmed the sky in the west with rays of gold slicing through fluffy cumulonimbus onto the valley floor. To the east, Mariam Bagulisha, a gently domed pinnacle of rock, soared from the flat ground to puncture the dreamy marshmallow sky. I felt that whatever I had been hoping to find in this country, this was it. I mean, this was really it. It was as if I was walking in the Garden of Eden, a natural paradise here on earth. I sat down with my laptop (I had rather stupidly brought it along for the trek) on my knees to jot down some notes and six children crowded around me. One of the older boys could read English and read out the words as I typed them.

They asked to see pictures and as none of them had been to Lalibela, I showed them some videos of the churches. A woman of approximately 70 years of age welcomed us into her house. Although we were planning to camp at a beautiful spot in the valley by an olive grove and water pump, we decided to accept her hospitality and stay the night. We ate *injera* and a delicious type of savory pancake with the *shiro* bean curd, sipping scolding sweet *buna* in the torchlight of a large whitewashed room. We washed our hands and feet afterwards outside in the courtyard next to a tethered cow. It was New Year's Eve, but I was asleep by nine o'clock on a small earthen platform raised off from the floor of the room.

In the morning, we set off through the patchwork valley to tackle the steep ascent to the church of Saint Abuna Abraham, the largest in the Gheralta Mountains. Located at the top of a sheer cliff, the church overlooks a long stretch of plain far below. Its interior is nothing short of magnificent; eleven huge pillars of rock soaring upwards to a vaulted ceiling covered in colourful 7th Century frescos showing the deeds of the famous local Saint Abuna Abraham himself. A priest, holding his wooden prayer stick and a metal rattle did a little prayer dance, murmuring intonations. Bennie translated: "God, I ask from you from my heart, that you give me good health and peace."

Descending, we fell in with two monks and several teenagers walking through a dry riverbed. One of the boys insisted on carrying my pack to demonstrate Ethiopian hospitality to travellers, and to show off to his friends. Dutifully carrying it down into the village he didn't allow the strain to show, although it is the only time I recall seeing a *Habasha* [a term used for an Ethiopian from the northerly regions of the country, which used to be called 'Abyssinia'] sweat. After a sneaky glass of *talla* at the local inn we walked along the plain which opened out into grassland; acacia and sycamore trees so delicately placed so that it looked like a Hollywood 'African' film set, with huge stalagmites of rock creating a cowboy backdrop.

We lounged under the largest sycamore tree, its incredible branches reaching out over fifteen metres from its huge twisting trunk. Birds of all kinds, colours and calls had flocked to this marvel, and it was a delicious feeling to lie in the long grass eating peanut butter sandwiches, listening to their chatter. That night I stayed at the house of Haile, a member of the guiding association in the Gheralta. He was not home when we arrived but his wife, Gabriel, took great care of me alongside her seven children, even though my arrival had not been pre-arranged. An impromptu English lesson began with her daughter Terhaus, an incredibly bright ten-year-old girl in the 4th grade, and her son Hamben, a twelve-year-old in the grade above.

They would scribble down words in English that I gave them: House. Cow. Mother. Light. I corrected the spelling and then they would write the words again on the back of the paper to prove they weren't cheating, although they often did, inviting squeals of remorse when I tickled them as punishment. Sheep pelts lay on seating and two flat raised areas served for beds. Decorative items hung from the walls: the single-stringed *masinko* instrument, skin gourds and colourful woven *injera* stands. These are handmade round tables weaved from straw but often with colourful trims, designed to keep freshly made *injera* off the ground. One item of luxury was a large gas lamp suspended from the ceiling, its tubing linked to a canister outside through the wall. This emanated a soft pleasant light over our classroom.

After we had eaten, all the children gathered around my bed. Hamben took down the *masinko* and played while the others clapped, led by their mother Gabriel. Terhaus did a little dance in the middle, wriggling her shoulders and stomping her feet. It was like a rendition from the Ethiopian version of the Vonn Trapp family, and I have to say my heart melted a little bit in my chest. In the morning Gabriel cooked me some eggs then made *buna*, carefully roasting the coffee beans and waving the smoke over my head as a blessing. She struck me as a happy woman despite the exhausting work of raising seven children.

Bennie came down from his house which wasn't far away, and we set off, the path leading us west through a valley between the cowboy mountains. We walked through some deep sand before coming to a green rush-filled stream where women were washing clothes and filling their yellow water containers. The path wound up the steep mountain above us where workers were in the process of building a large set of stone stairs leading up to a small church, perched halfway up the mountainside. Men were laying concrete to level the uneven stone floor, which seemed to me a gross error, albeit a practical one as they wanted to use the space for worship. I almost walked into a freshly laid section and was shooed away with laughter. All eyes were on me and I suddenly felt claustrophobic and made a beeline for the cave exit. I stopped in the doorway and turned back saying, *"Amisiginalo* [thank you], *salaam, ciao"* like some sort of awkward celebrity, before stepping into the sunlight.

A man offered to guide us over the highest mountain in Gheralta, into the next valley, which was fortunate as Bennie was unsure of the route. He was a humorous ex-soldier wearing an old camouflage jacket. He made the mistake of telling Bennie a 'funny' story of how he had overcharged some tourists for a few hours' work by taking them up to see a single church in the area. His smile faded somewhat as Bennie translated and I slowly nodded my head instead of laughing, realizing he had metaphorically shot himself in the foot in the hopes of over-payment for this day's excursion.

We set off up the mountain and the walk just got better and better. Soon we were well above the church, looking down to see it nestled in the side of the conical valley. Then we were up and out of it, striding past gigantic red faces of sandstone cliffs that led down into a deep river valley, a silvery snake of water in wide looping chicanes meandering off into the distance. We ascended to the plateaued summit of Mount Kemmer, the highest mountain in the region, a rectangular tabletop above his jumbled and unruly younger brothers; their peaks and curved promenades jostling and fighting for prominence below him.

I was reminded of the comment of one of the British soldiers under General Napier's 1867-8 campaign against the Emperor Tewodros II: "They tell us this is a table land. If it is, they have turned the table upside down and we are scrambling up and down the legs." It certainly felt like that as I slogged up in the midday sun, although the 360° view afforded from the top would have made it worthwhile twice over. We came down out of the sun and sat in the shade of an acacia growing next to a tiny hermitage, chiselled out from a domed anthill-like summit of stone. We ate small dry cakes and vacuum-packed dates imported from Saudi Arabia.

I opened the pack with a seven-inch Austrian army-issue *Glock* knife that I had on loan for this trip from my German friend Alex, its primary employment having been the spreading of peanut butter over sandwiches. Our scout's eyes flew to the object and he gave me an appreciative nod. I had noticed a fascination with the knife by nearly all of the locals who had seen it, many demanding to handle and play with it: for their rural way of life a tool of such practicality and workmanship being a prized possession. A thin walkway has been chiselled out around the side of the anthill, leading to a small locked metal doorway. A small circle in the exterior wall of stone acted as a window and through this I looked down to see the stomach-churning drop below, curving down and out to stalagmite spines of sandstone pillars jutting out from the desert like a dinosaur's tail.

Although easily exceeding a 50-storey building in height, from our position these pillars looked tiny in the heat-haze. Encased in the tallest of these pillars, about halfway up, was the most ostentatious of all the rock-hewn churches: Abu Yemata. To my right, a tiny hermit's cave had been cut into a sheer face of the table mountain. I couldn't help wondering who had chosen to live in there, and what, if any, revelations it had afforded them. After a long walk we eventually came down into a plain of farmland, parting with our guide and greeting a young boy goat-herding with his father. We reached the small village of Agoza, which means 'the skin of a sheep', and refilled our water bottles at a water pump surrounded by cacti and thorns on the edge of a dry sandy riverbed.

We walked across stony fields of red soil to the house of some of Bennie's wife's relations, where two sisters Yeshi, 17, and Abrihat, 19, live. They were both very pretty and we enjoyed sitting with them drinking *talla* beer then *buna* from freshly roasted coffee beans, eating our *injera* with the ever-present *shiro* bean curd. Their house was beautifully built with a twisted olive trunk as the main supporting pillar. I was told that their father had passed away around the time when Yeshi was born, and their mother, a strong looking woman called Nigisti, had raised them herself.

I asked Yeshi if she wanted to go to college and she said she had been working for a Chinese contractor building roads for a month to save money for this, but he had skipped town without paying her or any of the other workers. College started in February and it would now be very difficult for her to attend. Abrihat had a two-year-old daughter but was not married and there was no sign of the father. These trials and tribulations did not seem to be discussed as if being out of the ordinary.

With Bennie translating, I told them about what we had seen that day and asked Yeshi if she had explored many of the mountains. "How can we do that, without a *faranji* to take us there?" she replied. It was clear both sisters and their mother all wanted to move into a large town or city but were restricted by poverty. A steep climb led us out of the village the next morning, the path taking us up through cactus groves perched on the side of sheer red cliff faces, eagles gliding above us on the thermals. It was yet another completely new environment within the mountain chain and I couldn't help gasping at the wonder of the place.

We came around the last of these cliffs to an open spot and

stopped for lunch with a shepherd wearing an enormous cream turban like a snake charmer. We were at the northernmost edge of the chain now and I could see for miles across the desert plain to waves and waves of mountains in the distance, including the holy mountain of Axum, crashing upwards on the horizon in sharp grey bursts. We eventually descended to the church of Abuna Gabre Mickail Koraro, or, St. Michael's, Bennie having previously called ahead to the priest on his cellphone to come and unlock it for us. A relatively younger church, it was founded in the 17th Century by King Gabre Mesker. Nestled in the side of a sheer mountain cliff of light grey stone, parts of the exterior around its windows are been painted in a dark crimson. Tibetan images of Lhasa again flashed into my mind.

We entered and the frescos were the most impressive of all the churches I saw in the region. With a blue and yellow theme, they leapt out from the high vaulted ceilings and twelve delicate pillars in a cacophony of martyred saints: St. Peter having his head cut off; St. Jacob being stoned, his body filling up with large rocks; St. Paul skewered with numerous spears. All of them had their tongues poking out. Despite the rather gruesome subject matter, it was a calming place to sit in the cool away from the hot sun. We eventually headed down the mountain through a deep split in the rock, five storeys high and just wide enough for two men to descend abreast. We came across a beautiful camp spot in the lee of a huge natural cave in the mountainside next to a natural spring bubbling close to some small fort-like dry-stone ruins. I pitched our tent and we had a simple dinner.

A small dirt track led from the cave down to an acacia-dotted plain smouldering in the dying sunlight. In the morning we were collected by our minivan and driven around to the base of the dinosaur's tail we had seen from the summit two days previously. From the ground looking upwards it was a completely different experience and didn't look like a dinosaur's tail at all; more like a block of NYC high-rises in stone. I practically skipped up the short ascent to the base of pillars. It then became very steep to the point where I was climbing with ropes and was provided with a harness for a particularly tricky section. Upon reaching the top of a massive boulder, wedged about halfway up between the two largest stone towers, I met a small group of Spanish tourists. I chatted with their tour leader for a while, both of us equally rejoicing in the beauty of the mountains and bemoaning our fear of vertical heights.

During the late 5th Century, nine saints travelled as missionaries to Axum and were influential in the growth of Christianity in the region. Although legend has them all as Syrian in origin, many have been traced back to Constantinople, Anatolia and even Rome. Welcomed by King Ella Amida in Axum in the north, the son of the first Christian kings, the nine 'Syrian' saints then made their separate ways into the country, founding different churches and monasteries as they went. One of the nine, Saint Yemata Atan, came to Gheralta and legend has it that he rode his horse up the sheer wall to carve the church now named after him; his horse's hoofmarks still imprinted and visible in the stone.

From the top of the wedged boulder, we could see that windows of Abuna Yemata Atan Guh had been cut into the side of the largest pillar. To get inside, we had to shuffle along a metre-wide ledge with a sheer unprotected vertical drop of 250 metres. Ducking inside a small round hole, we were awarded with the cool, damp, mind-blowing interior of a place that shouldn't exist. For those unable or unwilling to make the climb there is the equally impressive option to visit the church of Abuna Mariyam Koko, which is a short drive from Abuna Yemata. The climb is more regular although I chose to do this particular ascent in the dark at four o'clock in the morning. The reason being that it was *Genna* [Ethiopian Christmas], and I wanted to see the holy mass that is performed throughout the night for the occasion.

After making the ascent to the church by torchlight, we were greeted by ten priests who were standing in the middle of the beautifully carved church. One of them was beating a huge leather drum covered with cowhide, held in place by a thick leather strap over his shoulder. He had a pointy beard like a Spanish Conquistador and did a little dance as he beat both ends loudly and rhythmically. The other priests stood around him in a circle singing and shaking their metal rattles in time. Waves of incense filled the air.

The music was hypnotic and through a microphone was played out from a round speaker wedged in a small hermitage window cut into the side of the mountain, the wailing prayers drifting down the 400m cliff face to the houses and farmsteads below. The service lasted all night, the priests taking turns to do readings or recite prayers, while others sat or snoozed on the wooden benches. One priest had given up completely and, fully wrapping himself in his shamma so that he looked like a leper, sat sleeping with his back against a large stone-carved pillar, his head between his knees.

I went outside at first light to watch the sunrise over the mountain chain next to the tannoy speaker, a priest in turn wailing like a Muezzin then praying very low and fast. The ledge I was standing on fell away in a perfectly vertical drop to the flat Tigrinya farmsteads on the tableland below. The Gheralta chain stood to attention like soldiers on morning parade. Before the sun rose over the horizon it ignited a small line of fluffy clouds directly in front of me in a searing coral through to gold, so bright I couldn't believe my eyes could take in a colour like that without burning. It was very cold. I waited for the sun to come up with my teeth chattering and the wail from the tannoy reverberating in my ears.

The industrious guide mentioned at the beginning of this chapter, Gebre and I, went on to build a trekking business in this region and I returned to here more than any other region in Ethiopia over the next five years. I bought twelve tents and stored them in Gebre's house, watched over by his wife and two young children, and we had many adventures together bringing tourists here, camping under the stars and dancing around campfires.

But at the time of writing in 2021, war has come to this place. The relatively small Tigrinya tribe from the north held power in Ethiopia from 1991, when Tigray People's Liberation Front (TPLF) rebels overthrew Mengistu's communist *Derg* regime in Addis Ababa. The Tigrinya then held all the major governmental positions until Abiy Ahmed Ali, from the far numerically superior Oromo tribe, became Ethiopia's Prime Minister in 2018. Although ending the 20-year post-war territorial stalemate between Ethiopia and Eritrea, tensions between Abiy's Ethiopian government and the TPLF erupted into all out warfare towards the end of 2020, greatly confused by the presence of Eritrean soldiers, with terrible reports of genocide, destruction, murder and rape on an enormous scale, making their way to the global press.

Gebre's house was looted then burnt to the ground alongside many others including tourist mountain lodges, with even reports that some of the churches had been destroyed in the area. His father, a 73 year-old priest, was murdered alongside his uncle, aunt and 30 others. We managed to get Gebre much needed funds after he had been hiding in the mountains for three months. For one of these months, he and his friends had nothing but a rotting carcass and leaves from the trees to eat. Thankfully his wife, children, grandmother and Gebre have now been able to escape to safety. But many families have not been so fortunate.

May God be with the people of Tigray.

9

KYRGYZSTAN: IF NOT ME WHO? (2017)

I was alone again. Really alone. I was in a valley camping next to a river and the air was rapidly cooling. I had filled up two aluminium water bottles from the torrent next to me, but the aggressive glacial waters made the liquid cloudy and gloopy. I realized this, emptied them, then walked over to a smaller stream cascading down from higher peaks, where the water was clear. The valley had long tapering pine trees that reached up to a sky filling up with twinkling stars. I had pitched my slim tent in the lee of a large boulder, away down from the track used by people and horses. As the light was fading, I looked up the steep grassy bank where I saw five young goats bouncing around.

I was boiling the water to cook macaroni. I'd also packed tomato sauce and a thick, fatty sausage that I cut into chunks with an army knife. I had walked for twelve hours that day on a radial hike to visit a glacier and my body was humming. While the water boiled, I focused on breathing in the chilly air and watching the stars slowly come out. The last wisps of cloud went purple. Time stopped and my mind stopped. There are just some moments you never forget. I had begun to run hiking trips in Ethiopia, but wanted to expand into a new destination, so I had flown to Kyrgyzstan to scope out the routes in the Tian Shan Mountains. These beautiful snowy summits run along the eastern border of this small Central Asian country, separating it from China.

I had been hiking along one of the more popular trails of the Tian Shan for about a week when I first met Maks on a wooden footbridge that forded a small river in a valley. He was leading a group of hikers but stopped to chat with me anyway, I think he was curious as to what I was doing there. A professional Kyrgyz mountain guide, he had a calm manner and smiling oval eyes which instantly won me over. He was due to climb Peak Palatka (4740m) in a few days' time with some Russian tourists, and I talked myself onto the advanced climb as a paying customer. I had done a huge amount of trekking in Ethiopia and other countries, but wanted to increase my skill level by taking on a more challenging climb. 'Palatka' means 'tent' in Russian. The twin peaks are so named because of their beautiful symmetrical shape resembling the old Soviet tents previously used by climbers in the region.

The Russian tourists ended up flaking out in the end, but we went ahead anyway, along with a local female Kyrgyz climber called Gulbara. Hiking and climbing are not popular with most of the men in Kyrgyzstan, and far less so with the women, making Gulbara a welcome anomaly. She is very beautiful, has a penchant for dressing up in traditional Kyrgyz dresses and taking photographs, and is extremely serious when it comes to mountains. I rented crampons, heavy winter climbing boots and an ice axe in Karakol, and we set out on the six-day round trip. A heavy snow was already falling. I remember pitching my one-man tent at our basecamp on the sloping side of a mountain. Two days later when I removed it, I realised that my body heat had seeped through my minus-20 down feather Nepalese sleeping bag, melting all the snow away. I had been so tired I hadn't even noticed I'd been sleeping on football-sized rocks.

Our little camp of two tents (Maks and Gulbara were sharing) was close to an impossibly steep cleft of ice that fell between two towers of stone like a frozen waterfall, at about a 70-degree angle. We had to hack out toe-holds with our crampons and use our ice axes to maintain a steady hold on the ice as we fought our way up. I was absolutely thrilled with the experience – this was real climbing. From the top of this we roped ourselves together as there were some hidden crevasses. The thickly fallen snow made this part of the mountain feel like some sort of ethereal wonderland, and I experienced a drug-like rush of endorphins.

We made our way in a looping curve up to a steep ridge. Maks was leading the way, I was behind him and Gulbara was behind me. All of a sudden we were in a heavy snowstorm and couldn't see more than two metres ahead of us. I could tell the altitude and conditions were affecting Gulbara, but she insisted she was fine and held it together, and we made steady progress. The snowstorm passed as we reached an area where the ridge levelled out a bit. At this height we could see impossibly vast rows upon rows of jagged shark-teeth mountains filing back to the horizons all around us, in great snowy barbs. But menacing dark clouds were rolling in fast from the north, looking worse than what we had already been through.

Maks pointed to the way ahead of us. We were only about 150m from the summit but it was up and over a knife-edge of a ridge that was covered in great sticky blobs of minutes-old fresh snow. Maks hesitated. I am no expert and tend to err on the side of recklessness, but I certainly felt that trying to go over that ridge in a snowstorm would be very dangerous indeed. Maks made the call and we headed back down. Gulbara was furious. The bad weather never hit us on the way down which exasperated Gulbara further and added to my own disappointment. But when we had made it safely down the ridiculously steep ice chute, the storm finally hit us. Even though we were only making our way across relatively flat ground retracing our footsteps, we became disorientated and could barely find our way back to our tents less than 100 metres away.

We eventually made it, although it took three times as long, and I was grateful we weren't still up on the exposed mountain. I always respected Maks for that decision, and we became business partners after that. I also stored tents I had flown in from the UK in his house in Karakol, and we began taking tourists hiking and horse riding through several routes in the Tian Shan. After a week back in the capital of Bishkek, juggling multiple work projects and my demanding Chinese accountant in London from my hotel room, I switched on the out-of-office on my email and got on a local bus to the countryside in the south. I wanted to scope out an itinerary that took in the great lakes and more of the nomadic Kyrgyz way of life.

After two hours or so, I woke up. We had stopped at one of the fast-food restaurant stops along the main highway, east of the city. I sleepily joined the queue with a tray to get some of the heavy meat filled dumplings called *manti,* and a bowl of spicy *udong* noodle soup. A young pretty girl with almond eyes stood in front of me. She said 'fast food' in English, which seemed a strong enough basis for us to sit down together at a table over lunch. Her name was Burulcha. She was going to turn eighteen in two days and was about to start studying Economics at Bishkek University. Her English was extremely limited, but we stuck to some very basic phrases as both my Russian and Kyrgyz are simply non-existent.

It was then that she came out with it: "What's your motto?"

I admitted that I didn't have one and, knowing that obviously she did, I asked her what hers was.

"If not me, who?" she replied.

It was indeed a great motto. I felt happy for her that she was so excited to begin studying, and embark upon a future full of possibilities. She was just the nicest girl I ever met.

I like taking local buses. It never fails to amaze me how much communication can be transferred without any knowledge of a corresponding language. In this way I passed the time chatting to three local women, taking the usual internationally applicable shit for being thirty-three and unmarried without children. From one nowhere town to another, I finally got to the last nowhere town closest to my destination. The skinniest of the three ladies (whom I liked the least) had kept telling me how far it was to where I was going and that I should stay with her that night, but I knew she was only doing it because she wanted money. She finally understood that I wasn't going to go for it and stopped trying.

When I got off the bus, I stood in the street surrounded

by men and waited for something to happen. One young man, more enterprising than his elders, stopped his car and in the street next to me, got out and showed me a price on his phone after hearing that I wished to go to Tash Rabat. We agreed a price and I got in. His girlfriend was in the back seat and came along for the ride. The journey was immense. After a long, flat plain filled with grass, the Tian Shan mountain range rose up in a steep, spiky-topped wall to my left as we headed south. After bombing down the road for about an hour, we turned left and drove into the mountains along a dirt track. The road threaded through weird and wonderful rock formations with long, green pastures leading up to the high places at a 45-degree angle.

We arrived at Tash Rabat, a stone-built Caravanserai on one of the ancient routes of the Silk Road, a two-day's walk from the Chinese border. Caravanserai were the inns of the ancient trade routes across Asia, where merchants could rest their caravans of animals, slaves and family members. A welcome relief from the elements and bandits, they afforded an opportunity to break bread, sing, and trade information and gossip in a multitude of tongues. I paid my driver, said goodbye to his girlfriend, and walked inside the damp interior of the domed complex, made from large rocks and cement. I knew from previous research that this building had been reconstructed by the Soviets, with even this relatively modern version beginning to be swallowed up by the ever-moving verdant mountainside.

'Yet as I looked in at the dark stable-rooms, used for housing horses and camels, water dripped in from the circular opening in the ceiling to release smoke from the cooking fires, I was sure I could ascertain the faint note of a lute, plucked somewhere from within the folds of history. I took my rucksack and walked up a steep foothill to get a view of the area. White yurt camps dotted the valley like fresh mushrooms. The valley was very green, and the river has fresh, drinkable water. It felt good to be back out of the city, and I enjoyed the wind and the sunshine. I was lucky to get a yurt to myself and slept soundly as the Milky Way sprawled overhead.

They had run out of horses in the valley the next day, as some large tour groups had come through and taken them up to the high pass with guides. I lightened my pack, leaving some things in the yurt as I would return that evening, and set off in the direction of China. I was glad to be walking in the sunshine. After a few hours the going got steep and the grass disappeared, replaced by grey slag and stone. I headed up to the high pass, breathing very heavily towards the top as the air thinned. On the other side the pass fell away down to the impressive Chatyr-Kul alpine lake at 3500 metres above sea level ['Celestial Lake' in Kyrgyz], 23 by 10km with glacial inflows, with the mountains of the Chinese border in the distance.

After eating a lunch of flatbread, dried fruit and nuts surreptitiously lifted from the breakfast table, I walked back to the yurt camp. In the morning the son of the camp's owners dropped me in the nearest town. His name was Rasul ['Prophet' in Arabic] and he was a teacher in a local school although currently off for the summer. He spoke good English and said he liked history and, when asked, said that his favourite part of Kyrgyz history was the Kyrgyz Empire. This period of self-rule and expansion preceded the Uyghur Empire (the Uyghur peoples of Western China share a much closer heritage with the Kyrgyz both genetically and in their practice of Islam than their Han Chinese rulers) and the domination by the Mongol hordes in the 13th Century.

He also explained that Tash Rabat had previously been a mercury mine (he actually said 'liquid iron' but I figured it out) until the Soviets had filled in the tunnels in the 1980s when they rebuilt the structure. I caught a bus to the nowhere town of Naryn. Opportunistic cab drivers who hang around bus stations tend to be arseholes all over the world, and my driver was no exception. After driving around aimlessly in town until a friend could come along for the ride, during which he constantly tried to re-negotiate the price until I ended up screaming at him and waving my fists in his face, we finally set off for Song Kol Lake. After he had picked up five litres of water from his house and played with his son. And bought some bread.

The drive was long and beautiful, going right into the heart of the mountains of central Kyrgyzstan. I started to appreciate it as the filthy mood he had put me into subsided. By the time we reached the lake I was spellbound with the beauty of the place. I didn't like the first yurt camp we stopped at. It just didn't feel right. When the old man saw that I was going to leave he told me that the next camp didn't have any water. That told me all I needed to know about him. "Yes, I'm sure we will all die of thirst tomorrow next to the largest freshwater lake in Kyrgyzstan," I actually spoke out loud to myself as we drove to the next camp. This one had good vibes with a young family and innumerable children running around.

I was given my own yurt and noticed that the small circle at the top of the roof had a modern touch with transparent plastic instead of the usual felt covering. This was swarming with about fifteen or so horseflies, which have a very painful bite. I wisely decided to worry about this later and went back out to ask for a horse. My horse arrived from another camp and after adjusting the length of the stirrups I rode out by myself onto the wide plain. The lake is enormous (270km²) and the plains surrounding it are also very large. It is big sky country and I spent a lot of time just watching the clouds drifting across it. Three young boys spread across two horses were shepherding a flock of about a hundred goats. I cantered up to them calling out the familiar 'As-salamu alaykum' ['Peace be upon you' in Arabic] which always puts people at ease.

The young boy who had a horse to himself came up alongside me and we spurred our horses into a gallop. He was riding without a saddle and of course completely licked me. Even without a saddle he sat effortlessly glued to his mount. His raggedy shirt was open revealing his brown tummy as tight as a drum. 'The horse is the true home of the nomad', I thought to myself. The previous week in Bishkek I was having a beer with a local history teacher called Jalil. He had grown up in the city and didn't get on a horse until he was twenty years old. He described the experience to me in these exact words: "It was like a machine I already knew how to operate. I knew which levers to pull – I instinctively knew how to control the horse and it felt like I should always have been there."

I explored the area around the camp for a couple of hours and returned home before sunset. There were two Kyrgyz families from two of the towns a few hours' drive away at the camp, and they invited me into the larger dining yurt for schnapps and *kemeys*, a slightly fermented milk drink. We did the usual round of international sign language and they gave me shit for not being married and being without children. I was right not to worry about the horseflies as when the temperature dropped with the sunset, they stopped buzzing and moving and didn't bother me at all in the night. Going to sleep looking at the wooden latticework of the yurt, I was very happy.

The next day I took a slightly larger horse out for four hours and explored to the west of the camp along the lake shore. Galloping free along the open plain was the stuff dreams are made of. It was very hot, so I tied a t-shirt around my head and wore sunglasses making me look like a kind of rubbish Lawrence of Arabia. It was quite boggy in places and I had to double-back a few times to find higher ground as I was very conscious of my horse damaging his legs in the uneven, watery ground. I rode up to the neighbouring yurt camp and they were also shepherding livestock and they waved to me.

When I dropped off the horse, the day was still young, so I walked four hours up and down the nearest peak, which still had patches of ice stuck to it. It drizzled just as I was reaching the top but then the cloud broke and sunlight dashed through creating a perfect rainbow. The lake stretched out before me and from this height I could see the wind play upon its surface. On the way down I heard some strange animal calls that I couldn't place. When I got down to one of the larger ice patches I saw a solo sandy camel standing next to it, which had been the cause of all the bellowing.

I had been lost in my own thoughts, but this snapped me out of my reverie back into my surroundings. Seeing a camel next to an ice field was a jarring impression (like imagining Hannibal bringing elephants over the Alps to attack Rome for example). I imagined it was very likely this camel's ancestors had navigated the perils of the Silk Roads, bringing profit to the generations of traders who for centuries have journeyed through the steppes of Central Asia. I was tired when I got back to camp but the family made me a shower with solar-powered hot water, which was an unforeseen luxury.

In the morning I hitchhiked around the lake to the northern shore but it was full of tourists watching some awful crap while a Kyrgyz girl dressed like Maid Marion shouted at them through a loudspeaker. I negotiated with a driver to take me to the nearest town, and after driving around for twenty minutes looking for other passengers, we drove off down the winding mountain roads. Then followed an exhausting day of travel via numerous buses, cars and taxis towards a yurt camp I wanted to see on the shore of Lake Issyk Kul. The largest lake in the country at 6200km^2, it is also the second largest alpine lake in the world after Lake Titicaca in Peru. When I finally got to the lake shore, I enjoyed its Mediterranean-like waters but didn't like the camp. It just didn't feel right, and despite my tiredness I decided not to stay.

I walked up to the dirt track and stuck my thumb out. The first car stopped. It had two large Kyrgyz women in the front seats, who turned out to be sisters. The one not driving was very animated and explained to me in Russian (I understood through her sign language) that she had been working at a health conference in Karakol selling products although she lived in Bishkek. For lack of anything more relatable to say I explained how much I liked *kemeys*, to which they completely lost their minds with enthusiasm and immediately invited me to join their family party. Tired or not tired you just don't say no to that. We arrived at their house, which was full of people. The two sisters were from a family of thirteen siblings – eight brothers and five sisters (how many times did they tell me this) – and they were all there.

In the main living room (this was a house not a yurt) tables had been placed together in a large 'L' shape, covered with white tablecloths. I was promptly seated at 'the head' of this and fed more slightly alcoholic milk than you would think it possible for one person to consume. One of the muscular sons of the siblings, who somehow explained he was an acrobat in a circus, refused to believe I couldn't speak Russian and constantly spoke to me loudly in Russian to the point where everyone just ignored him. Still, communication was possible. Among other things I explained that my grandmother was soon going to have her ninetieth birthday (I used the Kyrgyz numbers in the back of my phrasebook) and that she was German. This information was met with serious deliberation and respect by all.

One of the young girls was quite an actress and performed a poetic display in Kyrgyz, of which of course I didn't understand a word, but which was very entertaining. After about two hours I was so exhausted I explained I had to leave and after they dropped me in the centre of town I somehow found a taxi to take me to a guesthouse a few kilometres out as all the ones in town were full. This was a large building with spacious rooms and wide wooden stairs painted red. There were Kyrgyz families everywhere, but I had no capacity for interest in anyone else by this point.

I was given a large room on the ground floor with a thin mattress on a large rug. A bone bow made from the horns of a mountain Walia Ibex hung on the wall with a decorative arrow. There was an oil painting of an elderly Kyrgyz couple on another wall, the wrinkled man wearing the traditional hat of white felt called a *Kalpak*. As I lay there the wind blew in the thin white lace curtain out from the window and the breeze covered my legs. I thought that a lot can happen in a couple of weeks, and I thought about Burulcha's motto.

10

ETHIOPIA: THE TEMBIAN DEBACLE (2016)

What am I doing here?

– Arthur Rimbaud
(*writing home to France from Abyssinia*)

For a relatively short journey I had quite a lot of difficulties with this one. The Tembian Mountains are linked to the northern end of the Gheralta Mountain chain, running perpendicularly west at a right angle. They are practically untouched by tourists, with to my knowledge only one French company organizing about two trips a year through its remote plateau villages. The mountains are truly remote and difficult to access, with very long hikes required. The rock churches here are very few and do not even come close to the splendour of those in Gheralta, which accounts for tourism not having developed here.

Although I had been having some difficulty with Bennie, my guide in the Gheralta Mountains, he was one of the few English-speaking people in the area who knew the single route to access the Tembians, having accompanied one of the French expeditions as a porter. Unable to procure the services of a qualified guide, I reluctantly employed him for a second time to explore the range. I also hired a local scout, as although Bennie had done the trek before, I was coming to rely on what he told me less and less due to the weakness of his character. A minivan drove us to the unremarkable town of Tembian where we would begin the trek. On the way, we stopped at some orange groves to wait for our arranged scout to walk down from his village and join us.

The scout arrived. He was a handsome ex-soldier of the Eritrean wars, wearing a khaki jacket and sporting a cream turban. His name was Berhanu, and although not particularly aged in appearance, I named him 'Old Berhanu' in my mind and will henceforth refer to him by this name. Bennie suggested we should get some oranges, so Old Berhanu ran off into the grove and returned with his shamma full of green hard oranges. They were bitter and full of pips, but my body was grateful for the Vitamin C. We carried on to Tembian, where I paid the driver and opened negotiations for Old Berhanu's pay.

The trek was supposed to take three days to the town of Koraro, and I began haggling for the daily rate. Immediately I could see that Bennie was not cooperating in his role as translator, alternatively being sarcastic, sullen or simply refusing to translate on my behalf. We had already agreed on Bennie's fee, which was the same as the previous trek through the Gheralta, and he was making it very clear that although we had shaken on it he now wanted a raise, which I adamantly refused to give him. As soon as you start making concessions or go back on an agreement, a crack in the dam will be exploited by continuing torrents of demand.

Eventually we agreed on a fair price for Old Berhanu and set off. As soon as we left the town and entered the countryside, my stresses fell away and I basked in the glory of an immediately varied and interesting landscape. Walking up across a boulder-strewn river and through a grove of eucalyptus trees we entered a flat space flanked by small hills. Old Berhanu spoke and Bennie murmured that during the time of Mengitsu's Communist *Derg* control [1977-1987], they used to land helicopters here for soldiers to congregate for large meetings and celebrations. But upon further enquiries I couldn't get anything more from him.

'Don't push it,' I thought, instinctively knowing that making a scene in such an isolated place could only do more harm than good. I would save any form of confrontation until after we had finished the journey. I dropped back and enjoyed the steep climb up to a vast valley. I could see that Old Berhanu was certainly the man for the job. He was as spritely as a mountain goat and although he lacked the customary AK47, his iron-tipped *dula*, or shepherd's crook, and ties to the local people would prove to be more than sufficient to ensure our safe passage.

At one point, as I was walking along lost in thought, I suddenly saw him whirl, drop and hurl a stone into a scrubby tree just up in front of me. This was followed by a crash, then a slithering off into the undergrowth. "Snake," he said in one of his few words of English. 'Well,' I thought, 'at least someone is doing their job.' Upon gaining height the view was magnificent. The valley was vast, at least two kilometres across, with a glistening river curving through the wide plain. It had strange contours of rock that ribbed out of its side creating mini plateaux as if a giant hand had sewn them in place. Up in the far distance, an impossibly high village of spread-out tin roofs sparkled in the sunlight like water droplets in a field at sunrise.

We followed a path cut into the side of a ruddy cliff where ancient olive trees hung precariously from stone bases over the sheer drop to the valley floor below. We came to a level section and were greeted by a procession of seven villagers coming towards us. The man in front was holding a very large multi-coloured umbrella, looking like an advert for the Legal & General insurance company. He was followed by three women wearing white dresses, all with tightly braided hair, who bowed slightly upon our greeting. As we came up to a high ridge, we met a man and a young girl with seven or eight donkeys tightly bound with sacks of grain. On the other side of the ridge the land fell away to a vast desert, punctuated by rising ambas of rusty sandstone. The ridge continued upward, involving some gentle rock climbing which I took slowly, being made unsteady by my large pack.

We eventually reached the village of Abu Selama and I had to admit that I had never seen anything like it before. Instead of the classic dry stone, flat roofed Tigrinyan tukals I had become accustomed to, all of the houses were built in the round from a sturdy grey stone with beautiful large grass-thatched roofs. The proximity to the vast amba-filled plain gave the feeling that the village was somehow floating in the bright blue sky. An old man in a raggedy patchwork outfit who clearly knew Old Berhanu greeted us, and we were invited to his house for *talla*. His elderly, buck-toothed wife had a kind face and laid down a cowhide, polished with age and use, over the rock steps of their entranceway for us to sit on.

The old man wouldn't let my *talla* beaker go down any

further than halfway, as is customary, and eventually I had to stop him as I explained that I had had my fill the day before celebrating *Genna*. I used hand gestures to mime I had drunk up to my neck, which he found highly amusing. The couple pressed us with sour *injera*, but we were all too full up from our peanut butter sandwich lunch. Both of my companions nibbled tentatively at one corner to not give offence. We continued on to a collection of three tukals surrounded by a shoulder-high dry-stone wall topped with thorn-latticed fencing, creating an impregnable compound. Old Berhanu again knew the family and we were welcomed in for more *talla* and again had to refuse more food.

I could tell that I was really off the beaten path here as none of the children had been taught to beg, which is an endemic problem in much of the country. They simply stared at me in silence. We had to push Old Berhanu to leave as he was starting to enjoy his *talla* and friends a little too much. When we eventually got up to go, he had filled one of our empty water bottles full of the green yeasty liquid.

We descended through the village in the late afternoon and came upon an open stretch of cultivated fields. The path led down to a gorge of gigantic proportions. Orange and green tumbled down in rounded promenades of folding rock and forest. Perched over a sheer drop across the opening of the gorge sat the squat, freestanding church of Abu Selama, serene as a temple balancing on a mountain cloud in a Japanese *Ukiyo* [floating world] painting.

Here again communication broke down as Bennie declared that we would stay here for the night. I had been led to believe that it was going to take us seven hours to reach this point when in fact it had only taken four, including stops, and we still had two hours of daylight left. I decided to push on, as it seemed we could comfortably complete the trek in two days rather than three. We descended down the tumbling gorge into a jungly forest and it was nice to be in the shade. We joined a stream flanked by large boulders entwined in the roots of the tall vine-clad trees along the banks. It was fun to splash around the side of the water along the valley floor as the light lost its perspective when the sun started its final decent.

We followed the river out of the forest onto a plain and strolled along flat ground between acacia trees and termite hills as high as a man. The sun finally set in a gentle orange glow and I turned on my torch. After half an hour more we reached Old Berhanu's home and were welcomed by his young wife. We sat in the second of his buildings, which I had at first mistaken for a small church, while his young son danced around in front of us on the stone-hard earthen floor, and I was glad of this innocent distraction. Old Berhanu's wife gathered fresh coffee kernels grown on their land, grinding the husks off with a large stone on a curved basin of rock before picking out the beans and blowing the chaff from a flat wicker basket. She made hot, sweet *buna* and we ate *injera* with some sort of accompaniment although I have forgotten what it was.

I found out later that Old Berhanu's wife had commented that although I had a large body, I ate a small amount. Ethiopians, regardless of their naturally slim, wiry physique, can easily put away twice as much food as myself, even when I am at my most hungry. I made his wife a simple gift of a packet of dried sugar cakes and a pack of dates, which she enthusiastically accepted. I asked Bennie if she had tried dates before, but she understood me and said emphatically replied: "Yes". Old Berhanu offered me his bed but I refused. After dinner, I stretched my roll-mat out on the ground, unrolled my sleeping bag over it and immediately fell asleep fully clothed in front of everyone.

After waking me up at four in the morning, Old Berhanu went outside to loudly slaughter a chicken. I rolled over and went back to sleep. A couple of hours later I got up with the pale blue dawn and went to the toilet in a thorn-ringed enclosure outside of the compound. When I returned, we ate *injera* with pieces of the chicken in a stew poured over the top. We set off in the crisp, early light through a patchwork of rocky fields. It was impossible to get any meaningful information out of Bennie about distances or times or where we had options to spend the night should we need to.

The journey ended up taking ten hours, which although not any great disaster, is certainly longer than I would have planned. In truth I had no one to blame but myself, having gone against my own better judgment at the outset. I could no longer trust anything Bennie said, and so just bullishly pushed ahead to try and reach the end. After a couple of hours, we passed what was apparently supposed to be our campsite for the second night, situated next to a beautiful clump of trees surrounding a lush watering hole. Then began an unforgiving slog cutting diagonally up, across and onto a huge plateau.

I was hot and irritated when we reached the top, but the view calmed me down and I took on plenty of water in the baking heat. This was a day of vastness. The views were long and incalculable. I filmed much of the journey but upon reviewing the footage afterwards it looked like nothing at all; the camera unable to capture the scale of the open spaces, or the subtleties of the jagged mountain horizon. We passed by many homesteads and into a new wide valley below a large green-contoured mountain, guard dogs barking themselves hoarse as we passed close to their owner's homes.

In the Danakil Depression I had unwisely walked through the hot, salty, sulphuric water in my boots, and had latterly noticed that the rubber seal joining the sole to the leather of the boot had started to work itself away. I had not noticed the extent of the damage, however, as the corrosive water had seeped in under the left sole. This, combined with the baking heat of the sun and the stress of continued use over hard terrain, resulted in the glue completely eroding and the font half of my left sole flapping uncontrollably open, just as I was in the middle of a particularly tricky descent over a slippery sandstone rock face halfway down a huge arid rock valley.

"Ah, bollocks." I made it down with the sole flapping wildly but was unable to continue at any but the slowest of crawling paces. Old Berhanu ingeniously striped the bark from a young sapling to use as a cord to hold it in place but despite numerous modifications it would always slip off after ten metres or so. Fortunately, Bennie had a spare set of sandals and I put the left one on over my sock, which, although uncomfortably tight, was bearable. This natural sharing of resources did not soften my feelings towards him however; this trip had been a fiasco from start to finish. We continued on our way with myself, not having completely lost my sense of humour, appreciating the eccentricity of the situation.

"Sometimes when you are trekking bad things happen; you just have to welcome them with open arms," said Old Berhanu sagely in Tigrinya. We passed through numerous dry riverbeds, more giant termite hills, and forded a river before reaching the final plain in the twilight. The mountain stretch joining the Tembian and Gheralta chains rose up as an impenetrable wall of glowing amber on our right hand-side as our long walking shadows strode across them like giants in the setting sun. We continued on to the road by torchlight until we reached the small town of Koraro. I collapsed on the big double bed of a pension and again immediately fell asleep.

Bennie had indeed been right that this should have taken three days, but both trust and communication had totally broken down to the point where I believed nothing he told me anymore. In my mind (and not without good reason) his every word had become a lie to procure more money. This is a very dangerous situation to find oneself, especially in such a remote setting where I was at the mercy of both my surroundings and the local people.

In the morning I managed to temporarily fix my boot with a combination of tape and an old cord rag. Old Berhanu returned to his village after I paid him and Bennie tried to charge me an exorbitant amount of money for a taxi to take him back to the small village of Megab, our starting point. When I refused, he called a friend to pick him up on a motorbike. I paid him our agreed amount, and we parted with me making clear that I wouldn't be using him again in no uncertain terms. Then, as Bennie rode off into the distance on the back of the motorcycle, I, looking not unlike a hobo, walked back along the road for four hours to Megab. Young children hassled me the entire way begging for pens and money. Some of them threw stones at me until I started throwing them back.

When I reached the village, I sat in a small restaurant and drank an entire bottle of cold water straight off, then a Pepsi from a tin-capped glass bottle. 'Well,' I thought to myself, 'sometimes you eat the bar, and, sometimes, well, the bar, he eats you.' Never again would I try to save on money by employing an inferior guide. In the scheme of things, I had actually been lucky the way it had turned out, compared with the plethora of disasters that can befall a person in remote mountains. That was a lesson well learnt.

II

[IMPRESSIONS OF IRAN (2017)]

می نوش و به ماه بنگرو به تمام تمدن هایی که دیده است فکر کن

Drink wine and look at the moon
and think of all the civilisations
the moon has seen passing by.

– Omar Khayyám,
The Rubaiyat

My good friends Dom and Aida were getting married in Dubai
so I flew back from the UK for the wedding. Half the congregation on Dom's side were primarily British, and all of the
other half on Aida's side were Iranian. Aida's cousin, Alireza, a
dentist in Tehran, and I hit it off immediately. There is a picture
of us in some Dubai beach bar with Alireza on my shoulders.
By coincidence we are both wearing green shorts and a grey
T-shirt. Alireza and the family invited myself and some of
Dom's (and my) friends Daf and Rob to visit them in Iran to go
skiing, and we gladly accepted.

An amusing anecdote is that when I first flew into Iran for

this holiday, I only had a £5 note in my pocket. No one had told me that international banks don't work there and Alireza and Aida had to pay for my entire ski holiday and the duration of my stay in Tehran, until I was able to reimburse them upon my return to Dubai. We were welcomed into their homes like old friends. Alireza's gregarious personality ensures he is the principal music DJ amongst his friends when they throw parties. I dubbed him the 'DJ Dentist' which he found very amusing, and back in London I had this epithet engraved onto a silver money clip which I sent to Tehran as a thank you for his hospitality. I like to do my part for international relations.

We visited the palace of the Last Shah of Iran, Mohammad Reza Pahlavi. My first thought upon entering was: 'I bet this is what it feels like to shoot craps at the Monte Carlo casino in Baku'. The palace grounds are in the very north of Tehran, where the pollution isn't so bad and the mountains peek through the winter trees. All that remains of the many toppled monuments of the Shah are two giant bronze boots sticking out of the ground near the long concrete steps leading up to the ugly modern building. Gaudy French Rococo furniture, much of it mahogany, languished upon exquisite hand-stitched Persian rugs. The jarring contrast between East and West makes everything feel out of place beneath the outrageous cut glass chandeliers. There are priceless ill-fitting pieces of furniture from all over the world; gifts from Foreign Secretaries, oilmen, importers – anyone who wanted something.

Frescos of ancient Persian heroes adorn high circular ceilings with tigers and bows and arrows. There is a lot of marble. The effect is hotchpotch, wasteful, opulent, grotesque. I liked it. Celebrated war correspondent Robert Fisk recalls an anecdote when he went to dinner with a famous society lady in Tehran who was rumored to be one of the last Shah's last mistresses. Whenever the Shah wished to make love to a woman, she would be admitted via a side door of the palace to spend a few hours in one of the more discreet salons, and upon leaving she would be presented with a Labrador puppy, as a token of the King of King's affection. Just as he was concluding the dinner, Fisk was almost knocked down by an enthusiastic fully-grown golden Labrador, which burst upon him from the kitchen.

The artificial twinkling of the cut glass of the Shah's palace, however dazzling, was a mere foretaste of the majesty of the sun-drenched white-capped peaks of the Alborz Mountains. Rising up to the north of the capital Tehran, the high powder glistened with a bright white flashing beauty. I thought of when the protagonist dreams he is flying towards *The Snows of Kilimanjaro* in Hemingway's short story. My tiredness slipped away from me and I flew down as fast as I have ever gone on my rented snowboard, feeling close to the mountain. We had taken the high lift that had only just opened after a few days' closure, revealing the untouched powdery snow, with only the thinnest of icy membranes on its surface, whipped up by the wind.

The view from the top of the lift's exit point led across numerous snowy peaks to the perfectly symmetrical white form of Mount Damavand far in the distance. A potentially active stratovolcano, at 5600m it is the highest peak in Iran, and indeed the highest volcano in Asia. Unexpectedly the front edge of my snowboard dug in to what must have been a mogul under the surface, and I was flipped straight up and forward (I instinctively tucked my head down), bounced off my back – my momentum carrying my legs above me in an arc – whence I landed neatly in an upright position and continued downwards amidst a great scattering of lumps, flakes and crystals.

I could hear my friends whooping high above at my good fortune and, adrenaline really going now, I rolled from toe to heel in long lines to carve through the spray as a surfer picks his line through the best contours of a perfectly glassy wave. We joked about it afterwards down in the canteen below as we blew on the tops of our too-hot cups of coffee. As we bought these, we gestured to the waiter to write down the price as we spoke no Farsi. He obligingly did so, but in Farsi, at which the whole place erupted in hoots of derision and laughter from his colleagues. He went the colour of beetroot but laughed it off eventually.

Daf and Rob returned to the UK, and Dom and Aida to Dubai, but I chose to stay on and, contacting a local tour operator in Tehran that Aida used to work for, I employed a guide to hike to the fabled Assassins' castle of Alamut, that I had read about in Freya Stark's *The Valleys of the Assassins: and Other Persian Travels*. I was staying in Alireza's opulent apartment and, as is common in Iran, his parents lived in the apartment above. Upon hearing of my intentions, Alireza's father commented (in Farsi) that I knew my history.

After the Arabs had invaded the Aryan peoples of Persia under the banner of Islam, a new sect of the religion, known as the Ismailis, created strongholds of resistance to the Sunni majority in the high castles of the Alborz Mountains. This region boasts many heroes and stories; the most famous of which is Hassan-i Sabbah, the feared leader of the dreaded Assassins in the 11th Century. The word 'Assassin', first brought to Europe by the Christian Crusaders, is a corruption of 'Hashshashin' – the infamous garden where Hassan would bring his followers to bend their minds to his will. Plying them with hashish, he would allow them the pleasures of many women and sweetmeats, persuading them that they were in paradise.

Once removed from the garden, they would be told that they could only re-enter should they do his bidding, and willingly they were sent to murder Sunni Arab dignitaries, including the then Prime Minister of Persia. Hassan and his Assassins became the most feared rebels of the age. Hassan's castle Alamut, or 'Eagle's Nest', sits high up upon a strange dreamlike formation of volcanic black rock, which diagonally cuts up into the sky in thick lines of strata. It is a place of foreboding. Standing upon the foundations of the castle, which cling to the thin summit of the mountain, I surveyed the valley beneath me.

To the left a huge expanse of snow and ice rose up in overwhelming proportions. Below, flat metal roofs of smallholdings reflected the silver gold of the sun, which also bounced off from the river, cloud, cedar trees and everything else, hurting my eyes. Somewhere on my right a flag was fluttering. The air was fresh, the horizon long. I could smell ice in my nostrils. 'Now,' I heard myself think, 'this is somewhere.'

On the way back to Tehran I had stayed at my guide Hussain's family house. It was large and slightly run down. His mother suffered from mental health problems but was a most gracious host nevertheless, and we lounged in their vast carpeted living room eating from platters of fruit and sweetmeats. The room had faded yet beautiful embroidered rugs hanging from the walls alongside numerous family photographs and paintings. We slept Persian style which meant simply on the thickly carpeted floor of the living room on heavy mattresses with numerous duvets and blankets with a heater blasting in the centre of the room, and it was very cozy. In the morning I awoke to see Hussain bending over me. There was a silver tray holding two steaming glass cups of tea on the table. "You were sleeping so heavily I thought you were dead," he said innocently.

A few months later, I had just been refused entry onto a flight into Jeddah, the closest international airport to the holy city of Mecca in Saudi Arabia, from Dubai. I was on a freelance business trip producing a trade and renewable energy event in *The Kingdom*. It was 8am and I had just stepped off a connecting flight from London. I was tired. It was August, ten days before the Hajj begins; the annual religious holiday when over two million Muslims from across the world make the pilgrimage to Mecca where the Prophet Muhammad was born and lived for the first 52 years of his life.

The Hajj is the largest annual gathering of people in the world. Muslims walk seven times around the Kaaba, a cube-shaped building and the most sacred site in Islam: Bayt Allah, or House of God. I had a normal Saudi tourist visa (it had taken me five months to get the necessary invitation letter from inside *The Kingdom* to even apply for this) but the airline refused me entry because I didn't have a special 'Hajj Visa'. In the airline office my enacted whining/displays of outrage were completely ineffective and despite myself not being a Muslim, and them having already sold me a ticket, I realised it was just not going to happen. I bought another ticket to Riyadh, the capital, for the following day. On the plane the atmosphere was already different from the multicultural melting pot that is Dubai. There were quite a few Western-looking businessmen but no

Western women. The rest of the passengers were Saudis.

The Saudi women were all dressed in black burkas, the men in white dish-dash with either a large flowing white, or a red and white chequered headscarf, secured with black cord. The air smelled of camphor. From the TV screens and speakers a prayer from the Koran resonated, one that the Prophet Muhammad used to say before embarking on a journey, the gold Arabic script flowing across a video flying over clouds and a bright blue sky. I spent a day in Riyadh and a day in Dammam, a city on the east coast near Bahrain, before returning to Dubai. It was 45 degrees outside and the heat hit you like a furnace. It is an austere place yet I always find the local people extremely friendly, welcoming and helpful. Their mosques are built with a very understated style of architecture, a manifestation of Wahhabism, their stricter form of Islam.

You drive past endless desert; there are a lot of fast-food outlets; you meet American oilmen; you drink a lot of tea; people smoke in the public lavatories; you sweat through all your clothes; the women are covered from head to foot, very rarely revealing their faces, so you only catch glimpses of their flickering eyes. I spent two days in Dubai doing some work, then flew with Dom and Aida again to Tehran. We stayed at Aida's mother's large, stylishly decorated house, in a quieter quarter of the city. Tehran has a population of 15 million and although the traffic and pollution can be appalling, it has a great atmosphere: vibrant, chic, fun and completely removed from the rather stifling hard-line ambiance I had experienced only a few days previously.

Leafy tree-lined streets and opulent marble-fronted apartment buildings abound, with trendy restaurants and coffee shops on every corner in the richer northern neighbourhoods. Tehran was a welcome relief after a stressful and hectic week, and as I was now an 'old friend' for many of Aida's friends and family, a rather exhausting round of family parties ensued with everyone shouting over everyone else in Farsi across huge dinner tables laden with opulent platters of food, loud music blaring and dancing into the early morning hours.

Iranian women are extremely beautiful and although in public they are required to wear an abaya partially covering their heads, in the capital especially this is nearly always pushed as far back as possible, revealing their full hair and face often adorned with make-up and bright lipstick. At private parties in the houses of friends or family, women remove their abayas to reveal the most modern fashions (if they are rich of course). It is common for women to work but they still have many disadvantages to navigate in public society.

The men are handsome and some of them have excellent physiques as wrestling is the national sport. Sometimes you see a man walking down the street with arms like actual tree-trunks. If you meet an Iranian man for the first time there is a 50% chance his name will be Alireza. Both men and women have only very dark hair and olive skin from their Persian heritage. Some of the men have fantastically thick but well-trimmed beards. Iranians are not Arabs; they are descendants of the Persians and speak Farsi rather than Arabic. It is a completely different language (with a surprising amount of French and Spanish influence), although is written using the Arabic script.

The Persians, after creating one of the greatest empires the world has ever seen [553-330 BC] were conquered by the Arabs over a period of 20 years from the first attack in 633 AD, when Islam exploded out of Saudi Arabia after the death of the Prophet Muhammad. In bloody conquest, the Islamic Caliphates, under various dynasties, established an empire that ruled from India to Spain. The name 'Iran' only began to be used after the conquest of the Arabs, and derives from the word 'Aryan', denoting the Persians' ancestors' origin from the northern steppes of Central Asia and Russia.

Another fundamental difference is in the nature of their religion. Although Muslim, Iranians are Shiites, compared with the Saudis and indeed the majority of the Islamic world, who are Sunnis. The division in their religious beliefs stems from a division in the line of succession of the leaders of the faith after the Prophet Muhammad died. The Shiites believe that his true successor was Muhammad's nephew Ali who also married Muhammad's daughter Fatima, and the ensuing line of 'Imams' that followed from him until the 12th Imam 'Al-Mahdi' who disappeared after persecution by the Sunnis, and whom they believe will one day return again alongside Jesus Christ (also a prophet in Islam) to lead the Muslims in rightful governance.

The Sunnis on the other hand believe that Abu Bakr, close companion and through his daughter Aisha, the father-in-law of the Prophet Muhammad, was the true inheritor of the faith, and the ensuing line of 'Caliphs' that ruled after him. There are other myriad differences between the two sects, as well as many different offshoots and styles of Islam, but this is a basic explanation. They are all Muslims however, and Iranians and other Shiites will still make the Hajj pilgrimage to Mecca in predominantly Sunni Saudi Arabia.

We slept in in the mornings then would drive into the city to upmarket *chelo* kebab restaurants for lunch where it is good to be seen. The food is delicious, but the concentration of lamb and beef in huge quantities alongside buttered rice and thick yoghurt is so heavy, that often we had to return home for afternoon naps before heading out to see our friends again in the evenings. Dom and I decided to drive down to Isfahan for the sightseeing. The five-hour drive down from the capital passed through unbelievably dry, desolate and barren desert; a shock to the system after the mountain-enclosed, well-irrigated leafy streets of Tehran. It was difficult to believe that we were in the same country.

Yet as soon as we entered the suburbs of Isfahan, as if by a miracle trees reappeared everywhere in the shady, well-irrigated oasis of civilisation. Along the streets, as across the rest of the country, black and white photos of 'the martyrs' hung from lampposts. These are the men from local neighbourhoods who fought and died in the bloody Iran/Iraq war of 1980-1988, when Saddam Hussein invaded the western border of Iran, resulting in a catastrophic loss of life.

Isfahan, although the second largest city in the country, in no way compares with the frenetic energy of Tehran. It is much more subdued with more parks and far less traffic. The seat of the Safavid dynasty [1301-1736 AD] after the capital came down from the north, this era is considered one of the most important in the country's history, and the city's palaces and mosques are still the epicenter around which its daily life revolves.

We checked into a fancy hotel in the centre of town that in ancient times was also a Caravanserai [a rest-house for travelling camel caravans]. This was revamped into its current opulent, glittering manifestation under the rule of Mohammad Reza Pahlavi, the last Shah of Iran until his overthrow by the

Iranian Revolution in 1979. The main area of Isfahan, Naqsh-e Jahan Square, is 560 metres long by 160 metres wide, and is surrounded on all sides by two-story identically constructed buildings forming a perimeter wall. Before a fountain was built in the middle of this great space, nobles used to watch polo matches from the raised dais of Ali Qapu Palace balcony.

The square was and remains the centre of community life. The mosque, palace, hammam, bazaar, food halls, and peddlers' stalls all convene together to service the requirements of the people. Red-helmeted soldiers used to patrol the square, keeping the peace in the name of the king. European painters in the 17th Century were invited to come and paint frescos on the walls to demonstrate the ruler's treaties with the outside world. The great Shah Mosque, situated on the southern end of the square, is the jewel in the crown of the country. It is mainly blue in its outer mosaic colourings, and very large with two immensely tall minarets stretching up to the heavens, denoting its adherence to the Shia form of Islam, as Sunni mosques will have either one or four minarets.

The mosque contains four smaller mosques that enclose a communal courtyard where men would bring their camels to sell and trade, discuss religion and taxes. The dexterity of the design combined with the simplicity and scale of the architecture is impossible to relate. But they inspire the finer internal melodies hidden in the heart of a person, all-too rarely teased forth by the routines of daily life, and like a fine conductor, induces your soul to rise up and sing with joy to realise the heights of beauty which humanity is capable of attaining.

A mullah, seemingly of some importance, dressed in a light grey cloak with a dazzlingly white turban welcomed us and was very diplomatic in asking where we were from and explaining the teachings they do in the religious schools. These are found in the low-rise buildings that face the verdant gardens adjoining the main courtyard. He thanked us for coming to Iran and said that all people, no matter their religion or race, were welcome to come and visit the mosque, and he encouraged us to bring others in the future. I know a humble-brag or a fake smile when I see one, but he meant it and I liked him.

Outside the square, the royal palaces are situated between shady gardens and fountains. Features include: ceilings of cut glass; soaring wooden roof supports carved in the same style as the ancient stone pillars of Persepolis; the first mirror ever brought to the country at great expense from Venice; a draughty palace hall covered in frescos of various battles with Ottomans and diplomatic treaties with Uzbeks; a bed in which Queen Elizabeth II of England once slept but was so uncomfortable that Shah Reza Pahlavi ordered the hotel in which we were staying to be created; summer porches; winter porches with fireplaces; latticework windows; frescos of birds, flowers and Islamic patterns.

Dom caught a plane back to Dubai but again I stayed on alone and caught a bus the next day heading east, back into the barren desolation of arid nothingness, towards the city of Yazd. Yazd is quite remarkable because it doesn't seem natural for a city to thrive in the middle of a desert, yet it is one of the oldest towns on earth, with an estimated 2000 years of permanent human settlement. Set in the dead centre of Iran, it is the natural converging point of the country's trade. It is surrounded by a ring of sun-scorched mountains, with complex underground irrigation systems that keep the city alive throughout the blisteringly hot summers, when temperatures can reach up to 48 degrees.

It is famous for its windcatchers [*badgir* in Farsi]. A medieval form of air conditioning prevalent across the Middle East, these are a high, latticed chimney-like structure raised above a house or building to catch draughts of wind that are pulled down to cool the rooms below. They are very attractive to look at and many modern buildings across the region still incorporate them in their design. When I lived in Dubai for a couple of years, my modern apartment building was designed in this style. The *badgir* rise above the low-rise mud walls of which many of the buildings are still constructed. They are interspersed across the city by elegant turquoise-tiled domes and very tall, turquoise-tiled minarets.

At night I walked along the cooling streets to Masjid Jameh, the largest of the Mosques. I never feel threatened in Iran, day or night, and am less suspicious when first approached by men or women on the street, compared with some other countries, due to the Iranian people's natural inquisitiveness, and legendary hospitality. I listened while a mullah expounded on something in Farsi through a microphone, sat underneath a huge arched edifice bathed in white light. The men all sat around on red carpets drinking small cups of chai whilst the women sat outside in the courtyard on a raised dais, all in black abayas. An expansive looking man waved me over and insisted I share some saffron and pistachio cake with him.

The following day was baking hot and I lazed about. I went to the Zoroastrian fire temple but it was still closed so I sat opposite in a café working on my laptop for a couple of hours. Zoroastrianism is the ancient religion of Persia and when the

Arabs invaded, Yazd was one of the last strongholds of its believers, although many of its rituals and symbols have permeated into their religion today. At the great mosque in Isfahan for example, right where the King would pray towards Mecca, there is a beautiful green mosaic of the 'Tree of Life', which stems from Zoroastrian mythology. The Zoroastrians regard fire as a symbol of purity, and in the temple in a huge brass urn, pieces of almond and apricot wood are burning, maintaining a flame that has been kept alive for the last 1524 years. The temple was built by the Last Shah and so is relatively modern, but pleasingly understated.

Atop some simple pillars is the Zoroastrian symbol of a Persian man with an Achaemenid-era distinctive pointed beard, two large wings either side of him (one representing good, one bad) and a circle at the bottom, representing the consequences of one's actions. I went in to look at the flame then came back out and sat on a stone step in the blazing sunshine, the heat pounding away on my skin. I continued my solo journey to the bazaars of Shiraz, the region from where the grape vines of the famous wine originate from, and from there the ancient Persian capital of Persepolis. I will not attempt to wax-lyrical about the latter, because nothing I can say will do it justice. It is like trying to describe the Parthenon in Athens; all the clever prose in the world can't convey the feeling you have when presented with living history.

Alexander the Great burned Persepolis to the ground in 330 BC, destroying the Achaemenid Persian Empire following his victory over the Persian Emperor Darius III at the Battle of Gaugamela. There are varying accounts, but it is said that this was instigated by one of the Macedonian (Greek) courtesans, as payback for the burning of Athens by the Achaemenid Army of Xerxes generations before in 480 BC. Ironically its destruction preserved a huge amount of the exquisite limestone carvings of its foundations and pillars, which were buried for thousands of years beneath the ash and the sands of the surrounding desert.

By the early fifth century BC the Achaemenid Persian Empire ruled an estimated 44% of the human population on earth. The carvings at Persepolis portray representatives of the conquered vassal states bringing offerings to the Persian Emperors, not cowering as slaves, but as dignitaries dressed in their distinctive traditional clothing. A Persian carrying the staff of office with a dagger at his waist holds the hand of the leader of the Armenians; Assyrians follow with sheep; the Lydians carry vases, bowls, two metal armlets and are followed by two men with a two-horse chariot; the Scythians, marked by their pointed hats, bring a horse, and clothing including a pair of Scythian trousers; the Parthians, a two humped camel; the Ionian Greeks bring spices and ointments.

Hundreds of small hand-held clay tablets were unearthed on the site, many documenting trades in silver, others messages about everyday life, shopping lists, love letters. The cuneiform writings look like text messages on a mobile phone from 2500 years ago. Some of the pillars of the once great halls still stand to this day, each supporting the huge carved bulk of twin bulls at the top. All had to pass through the Gate of All Nations, protected by flanking carvings of the great mythological creatures Lamassus; bulls with the head of a bearded man, which originate from Babylonia to ward off evil. Truly, the interwoven impressions of Iran fill the soul until it overflows.

12

ETHIOPIA: TIMKAT AND THE FLOATING WORLD (2016)

After the 'Tembian Debacle' I decided to go it alone for my next trek. I felt confident enough in my understanding of the culture to get by unaided even in the remotest of areas, but I think mainly I just wanted some peace and quiet. Because of this and for several other reasons, this turned out to be one of my favourite treks. Having got my boots re-glued and stitched by a capable young cobbler in Axum, I headed down to Korem, the nearest town to Lake Hashinge. Korem is situated where the Tigrinya plateau first rises up from the Amhara plains, and, compared with most of the arid desert plateaux of Tigray, this first strip of highland is a lush breadbasket of green terraced barley and wheat fields.

The area today may contrast strongly with the associations many Westerners will have with the name 'Korem' as it flashed up on their TV screens for aid appeals during the 1983-5 famine of Ethiopia. What is not commonly known, is that the

Mengistu-led communist military dictatorship known as the *Derg*, used the famine as a counter-insurgency strategy against the Tigray People's Liberation Front (TPLF) guerrilla-soldiers, by further restricting food supplies, which of course also affected the local populace. Due to organized government policies that deliberately multiplied the effects of the famine, around 1.2 million people died in Ethiopia at this time, with the majority of the death tolls from the Tigray and Amhara regions of northern Ethiopia

The town was one of the early refugee camps of the famine, housing 35,500 children in April 1983, and witnessed appalling death tolls in 1984 until the BBC began reporting conditions in October of that year, prompting international assistance to improve conditions with further food aid. My trip was initially delayed due to illness. I have a long and somewhat tolerant relationship with diarrhoea, as having travelled to many countries where it is prevalent – alas often those that house high mountain ranges – I almost expect a bout as a matter of course. I was not particularly fazed therefore when I was taken with a rather nasty strain of the affliction the night before I was due to set off.

After numerous trips to the bathroom during the night and in the morning, I packed a light rucksack and set off at 7am to walk to the lake. After 30 minutes of walking over flat ground with a light pack I felt like I had walked for eight hours uphill carrying a refrigerator. I put my pack down and lay on it for a while, slowly admitting to myself that I was in fact rather ill. I limped back to the road and caught a *bajaj* to the dilapidated building that called itself a hotel. Three days later, after much rest, a strict diet of plain food with two kilograms of bananas a day for their potassium content, sixteen tablets of tinidazole, three of zinc and plenty of water, I bounced back along to the same track to the lakeshore.

The time spent holed up in bed was in fact highly fortuitous as it not only gave me a chance to get my notes from previous excursions in their first real order, it more importantly put me in the right place at the right time to view one of the most amazing spectacles the country has to offer, of which I was until then completely unaware. Under a cloud of disinterested apathy, I had barely registered some of the local young men putting up multi-coloured streamers across the street as I had ventured out early that morning to the pharmacy for more medicinal supplies. After a slow day of writing and reading I had just eaten my 27th banana and resigned myself to a mid-afternoon 'I've got nothing better to do' nap when all of a sudden, a huge caterwauling and clatter began emanating from the street outside.

I ran to the balcony and blinked incredulously as a huge shining procession of gilt umbrellas marched below me, twinkling gold and silver with reds, purples and blues darting flames in the sunlight. The entire street thronged with men, women and children all dressed in white. A hotchpotch militia guard in oddly assorted garments of khaki and camouflaged clothing wore darkly coloured shammas with varying models of plastic or polished wood-stocked Kalashnikovs slung across their shoulders, flanked either side of the clergy.

These were dressed in the most sumptuous robes imaginable, especially given the remoteness of the area, with red and purple velvets and soft green felt caps patterned with silver thread. Those not carrying the finely stitched parasols with

swaying tassels bore heavy wooden staffs with huge representa-
tions of the intricately latticed *Meskel* [Ethiopian Cross] worked
from chunks of brass or nickel, or carved directly from large
trunks of wood. My sickness haze evaporated immediately and I
rushed back to my room, threw on my boots, grabbed my video
gear and ran down and out the front door into the back-end of
the *Timket* [Epiphany] street parade. *Timket* is one of the most
important religious festivals in the country, commemorating the
baptism of Jesus Christ by John the Baptist in the River Jordan.

The main procession had already moved further down
along the main street of the town and I had to scramble past
vast multitudes of people on the left-hand side of the road,
almost getting flattened by a donkey cart in the process, where
there was just the tiniest amount of discernible space amongst
the heaving throng in order to squeeze past and catch up.
When I reached the main procession, I saw that excited young
men were laying down large swathes of red and gold carpet or
blue sacking, depending on what was immediately available.
Once walked across by the 50 or so priests, the carpets and
sacking were then re-rolled and carried down to the front of
the procession on the shoulders of the running men and boys,
to again be rolled open so the clergy's feet never touched the
ground. The boys' faces flushed with the excitement, exertion
and self-importance of a task being dutifully performed.

Then, as if a dam had broken on the right-hand-side of the
street, a huge shoal of human movement surged forward under
a forest of waving *dula* sticks, chanting and foot stomping. The
crowd somehow parted to make way for the group of men and
they stormed down the street as one body, stopping, forming
circles and dancing around and around in a whirling circle of

flying wooden sticks, then continuing on again. I ran up to them and angled my video camera above them pointing down to get a bird's-eye-view. None of them paid any real attention to me, lost in the ecstasy of the dance.

Nearby, men and women took turns in shouldering huge three-foot-long hide drums, smashing out a pounding rhythm whilst dancing around and around in small circles made by the crowds. Groups of young children in orange and white outfits with crosses on them, looking like miniature knights-errant, sang in groups. Young girls and old women crowded together in separate groups singing their own songs. Everyone was smiling, laughing and clapping. People closed up and left their shops to join the parade. Those who could speak English spoke to me, not of themselves but of the parade, as I was the only non-Ethiopian there. The procession ended with the entire town amassed on a large plain where the religious rituals could take place in a green canvas tent with crucifixes of a cream material crudely stitched onto its sides.

I climbed a hillside to get a better view of this hive of activity amidst the idyllic mountain scenery, surrounded by a swarm of young children. And then, as soon as it had begun, it was over; the white dots on the plain drifted back the way they had come and disappeared into their houses. I suddenly felt very tired and trudged back to bed.

The only lake of any size in Tigray, Hashinge feels like the Como of Ethiopia. It joins two large areas of lush flatland to the north and south where droves of cattle and other livestock are brought to graze and water. At a 2500m elevation the lake waters rest calmly, enclosed to the east and west by beautifully terraced foothills.

A church flashed like an aquamarine stone on a hillside as the sunlight caught it, the rays then abruptly cut off by an angry cloud rolling in to the higher peaks. I walked west along the south side of the lake, enjoying the shading of the water created by the rippling breeze, greeted by shepherds herding huge-horned cattle coming the other way. My plan was to walk up into the mountains on the west side of the lake, head north for two days, come down into the small town of Maychew, then summit Mt. Tsibet, situated to the northwest of the town at 3935m. It is the highest in mountain in Tigray. I had not heard of anyone doing the walk and didn't bring a tent, assuming there would be plenty of mountain villages there upon whose hospitality I could rely.

The walk up into the foothills through grass-thatched villages was beautiful. The lake shimmered on my right hand side and everything was green. I passed a group of a hundred or so men all sitting down by a barn, celebrating the back-end of *Timket*. The hills became mountains and undulated higher. Passing through one village I was suddenly confronted with two huge glossy-coated yellow dogs, or curs, the size of small bears, running towards me at a frightening speed frothing, growling and barking. The first to reach the dirt bank was just about to leap off on to me (I saw his head go down for the pounce) but I had quickly dropped, picked up a large rock and, holding it high in the air so he could see it in a throwing action and making my body large, I gave the loudest grizzled growl I could manage.

This was just enough to check his leap and also that of his companion, and I slowly backed-up off the track across a field. They were only doing their job but I was positive they would have gone for me if I hadn't reacted. At my next water stop I strapped my knife to the outside of my belt for the first time. Just in case. I also knew there were hyenas in the area and it gave me a surprising amount of confidence. At the next village I asked for water, for which they refused the offer of payment. The girls wore multi-coloured beads woven into their dresses, their timelessly consistent style of hair braided back to the middle of the head, then exploding out in large and frizzy plumes. They were a friendly family and I had to disentangle myself from them as it was still early in the day and they were trying to get me to sit on one of the small hide stools which had miraculously appeared and eat *injera*.

The father held my hand as he walked me out of the brushwood-fenced compound and they all yelled and directed me up the next mountain onto the correct path, which I had missed. The local track took me up and up until I came down into peaceful pastures with gnarled and twisted yew trees, providing occasional shade in the otherwise open, contoured grassland. Passing through a couple of villages I reached a deep terraced valley, at its head a large mountain crowned with four rocky peaks. All of the locals had said that if I wanted to reach Maychew I had to go down, onto and across the plain – advice I completely ignored.

I spotted a small grassy pass in the shape of a 'U' just to the left of the four peaks and my nose told me to head for it. I passed around the perimeter of one village seemingly deserted apart from a lone snotty-nosed baby girl. I passed through another gauntlet of dogs, and although losing the track, headed up to the pass. I saw some women bent double carrying heavy bundles of firewood high up above me on a perpendicular heading. I started to feel the altitude for the first time and dragged my heavy legs up to the top. The view down on the other side was spectacular. An easy path through grassy woodland followed, as I had hoped it would, down and around the back of the four peaks on the right of the valley. On the other far side of the valley a tightly clustered village of thatched roofs on a small ledge looked like a mushroom patch in the distance.

Ahead, ruddy mountain passes dipped, then rose up as impenetrable walls, their summits leading to further hazier summits, backed up against the horizon. I passed some children herding their animals and followed the long path down and to the right, passing through more tiny hamlets. At one of these I saw a girl in an orange dress with her face painted a bright orange, from what I assumed must have been henna. Just as I was getting tired I reached a shallow green valley with a water pump half way up it, with large gusts of cloud rolling in and settling down from the east. A man in the last hamlet had gestured for me to take a left up over a small hill when I reached it. Somehow I felt that this was the last stretch of the day and sure enough as I rounded the crest of the hill and came down into another lush terraced valley I met a priest and he guided me into a grass hut compound.

A woman in her thirties owned the house and when I gestured if I could sleep there she gave me a look as if I had just asked her if it was OK if I breathed oxygen. Her mother lived with her and there were four young children running about. When she brought out the *injera*, the priest and his young novice stood up and, with a small metal cross in his hands, the priest intoned and prayed over the food with the novice saying prayers at certain intervals. I stood up and made the sign of the cross to show them I was part of the gang for reassurance and bowed my head. I remained in this position for a good ten minutes. The priest then splashed some water around the whitewashed dung walls of the tin-roofed hut, and we finally sat down to eat the flatbread with a hot red paste made from the spice *mita-mita* which I have not come across in any other country.

Communication was limited although, a picture worth a thousand words, I showed them some photos from my trip on my iPhone, eventually coming to photos from England. I had taken a picture of a dark blue 1960s Rolls Royce Silver Cloud in Mayfair for a friend of mine who is something of a Roller aficionado (although I watched him doughnut one in an empty dirt parking lot in Dubai one time), and I don't mind admitting to you that to these innocent farmer-folk and men of the cloth, I pretended that this was my car. I actually overheard the grandmother talking about my *makina* to another round of priests who came in for food later.

It seemed to be a hotspot for the clergy to dine, although I never saw payment exchanged. Despite the language barrier we actually had a bit of a laugh together with me mimicking the parade for *Timket* in Korem, banging large drums, carrying crosses, whooping around with *dula* and so on. They gave me a comfortable bed in a partitioned-off storeroom and I fell asleep listening to the children playing and giggling. You could see in their eyes that they were good people. I was very aware of the amount of trust they had placed in me. I was a complete stranger to them, an uninvited foreigner with no references. Yet here I was welcomed to sleep in a house comprised of only women and children. I found the circumstance strangely touching.

In the morning after a wash and some food I had to fight

the mother tooth and nail for her to accept payment, which she
didn't, so I ended up just leaving it on a bench. I was escorted
out of the village by a collection of five or so priests and about
the same number of men carrying machine guns for show. I
found out later that the last foreigner to come to this village
before me had been an aid worker two years previously. The
path continued up to an even higher pass and after about an
hour I reached the top. A tiny climb brought me to a small
summit and I looked down into a huge valley stretching out in
a never-ending sea of soft cotton wool, as I was way above the
cloud line. Back the way I had come the cloud had also settled
over the valley with the water pump. I took off my T-shirt and
basked in the warm sun, my flea-battered white skin soaking up
the Vitamin D.

I could hear the strange whoops and calls of hyenas from
up and across a rock-strewn green section of mountain, but
I couldn't see them. The long descent brought me through
another village settled on a promenade just nestled above the
cloud, which in my mind I named 'Laputa' after the floating
island in Jonathan Swift's *Gulliver's Travels*, I continued down
down down amidst idyllic scenery for most of the day to soft
green plains where men where ploughing with oxen. When I
finally reached the tarmac road, I hitched a ride into Maychew
past the Raya Brewery from a rich local family driving a cam-
ouflage-painted Toyota pickup.

This sleepy backwater town has a surprising amount of
historical significance. The Battle of Maychew [March 1936]
was the last major battle fought on the northern front under
Ethiopian Emperor Haile Selassie before he was forced to flee
the country to the UK during the Second Italo-Abyssinian War.

Mussolini, through his Marshal Pietro Badoglio, employed the lethal weapon of mustard gas more heavily here than in other battles, and six weeks later his troops marched unopposed into Addis Ababa. Haile Selassie re-entered Addis in May 1941 as a combination of British, Commonwealth, Free French, Free Belgian and Ethiopian forces liberated Ethiopia from Italian control that year, due to Mussolini's siding with Hitler at the beginning of the Second World War.

Maychew also saw significant resistance fighting during the Ethiopian Civil War, when the Tigray People's Liberation Front (TPLF) and the Ethiopian People's Revolutionary Democratic Front (EPRDF), a coalition of rebel groups, overthrew Mengistu's Marxist *Derg* regime in 1991. A tapering stone obelisk stands on one of the hills overlooking the town in remembrance of those rebels who lost their lives in the conflict.

The next morning, after a night in another flea-infested hotel, I headed out from Maychew towards Tsibet, cutting directly across the countryside until I came to its foot. I had met with two interesting Habasha men home for the holidays the previous evening, both working for the UN with South Sudanese refugees and, becoming engrossed in political discussions, we had certainly consumed one-too-many glasses of ouzo. The fresh air was doing me good and I looked forward to a stiff climb. Following a steep track, after a couple of hours I came out onto a beautiful grassy meadow surrounded by yew trees. The meadow was large and extremely peaceful and in my mind I bookmarked it for a future campsite, although I have never returned here.

I stopped in the meadow for a while to bathe in the sunlight, watching the country traffic pass to and fro. Quite a few men were riding horses and cut dashing figures with their shammas blowing in the wind as they galloped across the plain. Green tree-covered mountains rose up all around with villages and hamlets dotted everywhere. I headed through a forest, then a large village, on a path that led up to the high grasslands. Coming around the east side of the mountain, its grey battlements arose up above me menacingly. I followed a track up and through the last village, with a particularly ferocious dog gauntlet, coming to what I later termed 'The Chute of Misery'. The only break in the vertical stone faces of the southern side; a thin natural chute led up into the mountain. About 20m across, it rose for 300m at a clean 50 degree angle.

In combination with the altitude, I felt my pace slow to a trudge as I put my mind in a happy place and just let my feet do the work. A young shepherd sat on a rock at the bottom of the chute listening to a box radio, the repetitive beat of the songs reverberating from the rock walls. When I finally reached the top, I followed some excellent ridge walking along a col towards the summit. This was not much higher than the col and is formed, unexpectedly, of a soft grassy mound of such perfect proportions it reminded me of an Iron Age hill fort. Bouncing up the grass with renewed energy it was by far the most rewarding summit of my trip, and its 360 degree view one of the most moving in terms of grandeur.

I had that feeling that you don't always get but when you do get it you remember why you climb mountains. To the north, greenness left the plateaux as it ventured further into Tigray, its dusty dry peaks enveloping one another, somehow emanating a biblical, holy feeling. To the far east the land dropped away in a sheer fall of at least a thousand metres to a frying pan plain, eventually leading to a thin-walled cordillera; the perimeter of the dreaded Afar region. To the south and west the green-topped peaks had become silvery blue in the haze of distance and I traced my route from the preceding days. Directly below and four hours up, the grassy meadow I had walked across was etched by the straight line of the dirt track, bridging the curve of a small stream like a crossbow.

Maychew glinted like silver powder. Above me the sun caught the edge of a thin curling wisp of cloud and it flashed golden against the blue. I flung up my arms and gave a great yell to the gods.

13

AUTUMN IN MONGOLIA (2018)

"Lunch!" The heavy clumping of boots over crisp sun-dried grass woke me from a deep sleep. I was in my sleeping bag on a simple wooden bed and the book I had been reading had fallen face down onto my chest. I was in a large *ger*, the traditional round felt tents used for thousands of years by nomadic people, and all I wanted to do was sleep. As I pulled on my boots my eyes lazily roamed over the ornate array of family photos, keepsakes, and a Tibetan Buddhist shrine. Delicate paintwork on orange wooden slats led up to the circular band of wood at the top of the roof, its canvas flap half open with the metal chimney from the woodstove poking out.

It was October and it had already been a hell of a year. The company was expanding rapidly and in the last couple of months I had been approaching burn-out as the constant manic pace of keeping up with everything had started to wear me down. This was the life I had always wanted but I hadn't had a holiday in more than thirteen months, and I needed some space to regroup and recharge. Although this was technically a research trip, I was hoping it could double as some much-needed time out.

It had always been a dream of mine to go to Mongolia, but as I stepped outside, blinking into the dazzling sunlight of the steppe, and trudged over to the other *ger*, I didn't even feel like I was here. My head was still buzzing with a thousand stresses and worries, cutting remarks people had made, and a general perspective of negativity that exhaustion tends to bring on, which the long sleepless flights from London and Moscow had done nothing to eradicate. After lunch I was back in my sleeping bag absorbed in my book until Mogi, my driver, popped his head through the door and indicated that we were going to go and drive somewhere. I couldn't even remember what we were supposed to do that day. "OK I'm coming".

I climbed into the passenger side of the Hyundai 4x4 and we sped off across the rolling brown plains. I had purposely chosen not to have an English-speaking guide and was especially glad of this now as we rode along in comfortable silence, the vast horizons hinting they could make some dent in the unseen whirligig of thoughts clouding my mind. It turned out we were driving into Khustai National Park to see wild horses known as *takhi*; the only wild horse to survive in modern times. It didn't take long before we got up close to a herd, and we stepped out of the car into a biting wind to watch them silently going about their business. Also widely known as Przewalski Horses, their backs are a warm russet that fades to a light calico on their bellies and legs.

Their necks seemed more pronounced and the feeling I got from the herd was the same as being amongst a dazzle of Zebra in Kenya earlier that year where I had been leading a trip. At the time I had asked our Maasai guide: "Why did the Maasai never ride the Zebra?" He had just laughed and said: "You try getting on one". Mogi indicated that I could walk up the steep hill to get closer to the herd if I wanted, so I took a bottle of water and started trudging up. Once I started moving in the sunshine, the wind lost its edge and I had to take my coat off. It felt good to be getting some exercise.

I gave the herd a wide berth because I had no experience with these wild animals and headed on up to a small summit. At the top I thankfully gulped in the cool air and stared out at the southerly blue/brown puttied waves of foothills thrown up en route to the horizon, which lead to China. It was only just now starting to sink in where I was. Mongolia is situated between Northern China and Russia's Siberian tundra. In the west it is separated by just 50km from the border and the great swathes of Kazakhstan, whose people also used to be nomadic pastoralists, by the clamping jaws of China and Russia. Roughly speaking the natural topography of the country from north to south is in three bands: thick forest, steppe grasslands and the sandy deserts of the Gobi.

In Mongolia's west the land rises to the Altai Mountains, which cradle the vast steppe of Central Asia all the way to the Carpathian Mountains in Ukraine, beyond which lies Hungary and the start of Europe. We were in Övörkhangai Aimag [Province] to the southwest of Töv Aimag, which houses Ulaanbaatar (Red Warrior), the huge sprawling capital city. The next day we were speeding down an asphalt road through more of the endless putty hills and plains full of horses and livestock. If a nomad owns *tavai tolgoi mal* [a five animal herd] of sheep, goat, camel, horse and yak/cattle he is considered wealthy. The lives of the nomads revolve around their livestock, which is the main reason for their life of constant movement; the never-ending need to find fresh pasture throughout the unforgiving seasons.

The sky was a bright clear blue and I was reading. We eventually pulled into the small town of Kharkhorin (also known as Karakorum) and stopped outside its museum. In the 13th Century Genghis Khan had united the Mongol tribes and exploded out of the country to create what would grow under his descendants to be the largest empire the world has ever seen, stretching from the Sea of Japan to the Danube in Hungary. He founded the cosmopolitan city of Kharkhorin as his capital although it was later moved to Peking by his grandson Kubilai Khan.

Just as impressive as the military prowess of the Mongols was the ability of their rulers to transition from conquering and pillaging to government and administration. The taxes levied by the empire were largely used to serve the diverse peoples they ruled, partly by promoting the arts. Highly tolerant of most religions, they created the first stable trade and communication routes across Eurasia which enabled the first direct relations between China and Europe. Still, you didn't want to be on the conquering end of the machine when Mongol horsemen and their deadly arrows would destroy entire cities, slaughtering whole populations in order to instill fear and break the resolve to fight in the surrounding regions. In the 16th Century, Erdene Zuu Tibetan Buddhist Monastery was built on the ruins of the city.

Surrounded by monumental walls and 108 white stupas, beautifully preserved temples supported heavy sunken roofs of glazed tile and painted wood. Monks could be heard chanting with some standing around outside clad in their flowing robes in the cold sunshine, smoking. The spin of prayer wheels creaked in the wind and a few locals were seeking advice and teachings in a large ger. We drove further west in the morning off the asphalt road. We arrived at two *gers* and a nice lady called Sama greeted us with a blue scarf held out below a bowl of milk tea, which we both drank from, acknowledging her welcome.

She cooked *tsuivan* [meat with steamed noodles] over the wood-burning stove. Once we'd gulped down the food, a mute man who only communicated with hand gestures brought two stout horses for Mogi and I. Mogi, a 53-year old father of three, looked and dressed like a regular guy. But for our ride he'd donned a beautiful burgundy *deel*, the heavy finely-woven brocade overcoat that fastens at the shoulder and comes down to below the knee, with a bright yellow *buss*, the sash tied around the waist, and fine knee-high leather boots. The effect completely transformed him from a 'Regular Joe' into a proud, honourable man emanating an indefinable sense of calm. I noticed he carried himself differently in his *deel* as did all the local nomadic people I met, who often looked downright scruffy in their dirty Western clothing. Once they donned their *deels* (no matter how dirty or torn), they were transformed into timeless versions of their best selves.

Mogi spoke about 25 words of English and had begun teaching me Mongolian along the way to pass the time. There are two types of horses in Mongolia: one is *nomkhon* – quiet and good-natured, and the other is *zhang hai* – wild and fiery. It was evident within the first five minutes that my horse was a *nomkhon* – closely bordering on unconscious. He was also quite *daban* [fat] and I resigned myself to not having any real horsey fun on this ride. But it was no matter. Mogi led the way through a larch forest burning with autumn shades and we began to ascend a small rocky mountain, albeit the highest in the area. We tied our horses on a rope suspended between two trees and I immediately sensed that we had come to somewhere special.

We stood staring up at Tuvkhun Monastery, where Zanabazar, the head and founder of Mongolian Buddhism, had lived and created his famous artworks in the 16th Century. I took off my chaps and we walked up the rocky path to a small collection of temples. A man and a younger man and women were assembling a winter ger, washing the bright red painted wooden poles before constructing the framework. It was more the feeling of the place than the temples themselves that resonated with me. We climbed up to just below the top of the rock summit. There Mogi showed me the famous 'cave of the womb' and how to pull oneself into a minuscule crawlspace burrowed into the rock, turn around (with great difficulty) and then crawl out again to be 'reborn'. I had crawled in a short way when claustrophobia hit me like a knife in the gut and I pulled straight out of there.

"Mogi, there is no way in The Lord's holy trousers I'm going in there – let's go up top."

Mogi chuckled our way to the top and we walked onto the flat summit that had a round *ovoo* [cairn] of stones supporting a wooden pole with blue and yellow silk scarfs fluttering in the breeze. We walked around the *ovoo* three times, throwing loose rocks and pebbles back up onto the mound. The 360 degree view around us was of green turning gold larch trees growing in perfectly regulated straight lines, leading to rusty foothill rollers with cloud shadows moving across them.

We rode the horses back down to the *gers* and I watched two men from the camp, one on a horse and one on a motorbike, corral their large flock of goats sprawled up one side of the valley. For the cattle and yaks, they just rounded up the young calves into a small pen close to the *gers* and the herd instinctively stayed around them. The many horses were added to the ever-growing herd as both the light and temperature began to plummet. I thought how wonderful it was that these species could cooperate with such serenity. This fantasy was rudely disbanded almost immediately as the horses swiftly began booting and biting each other, the cattle and anything else within range. They didn't settle down properly until it was fully dark.

Later that night I wriggled out of my sleeping bag to take a pee in the night and gazed up in awe at the Milky Way sprawled majestically across the night sky, larger than my eyes could take in at once. I began to map out the constellations. To the northwest, Hercules danced like a hyperactive spider into the pots and pans of Ursa Major and Minor and the 'North Star' Polaris. Orion I deemed the 'warrior lobster' in the south. The five stars of Auriga I imagined as a boy-band because its brightest star is Capella. There was more: the great square of Pegasus; the twin stars Castor and Pollux of the Gemini constellation; and the 'seven sisters' of the Pleiades, the seven daughters of Atlas – the Titan of Greek mythology who holds up the sky. I couldn't for the life of me pick out the jagged scrawl of Cassiopeia, but soon gave up because I got too cold and crawled back into bed.

After a short drive we reached where the Ulaan Tsutgalan River [Red Confluence] meets the Orkhon River in a roaring waterfall. It was here in the Orkhon valley that Ghengis Khan in 1204 as ruler of the eastern tribes of Mongolia defeated his powerful enemies in the west, the Naiman tribe, led by Tayang Khan. Although greatly outnumbered he employed tactics that would become associated with the Mongol Empire for centuries by ordering that every man light several bonfires at night to fool the enemy as to the true size of his army. He lured the Naimans to a pitched battle when Tayang's son Kuchlug convinced his father that to retreat to the safety of the Altai Mountains would be an act of cowardice. Following this fatal decision, the Naimans were heavily defeated. At the age of 43 Genghis sat astride the banks of the Orkhon as the ruler of all the Mongol tribes, with the world at the feet of his horse.

It turned out that we didn't really have much to do that day, so we drove out to a stretch of the river. As Mogi cast his fishing line into the milky waters, I sat on a warm stone in the sun with my head on my knees and read about the manifold atrocities inflicted upon the nomadic peoples of Central Asia, first by the Russian Empire, then the rise and fall of the Soviet Union. Mongolia, more than any other post-Soviet state, has been able to return to its nomadic heritage and way of life, which the USSR forcibly undertook to eradicate across the myriad Central Asian peoples. It was sobering reading.

I was dozing off in our *ger* when Mogi came in with Bataa, my guide and horseman for the next four days. Aged 39 years old with high tanned cheekbones and a measured expression, he was dressed in a splendid turquoise *deel* with a bright orange *buss*, over which he wore a high-collared silk Chinese jacket embroidered with gold dragons and a thick navy-blue Communist-style peaked cap with 'Sport' embossed on the side in copper. It was quite the entrance. Mogi and I had already consumed quite a lot of vodka that night but Bataa insisted that I play them a few tunes on my fiddle which I had brought with me. Where Mogi had an inquisitive mind when it came to the English language, Bataa had none. The only words I heard him utter in four days in the language were 'yak' and 'ok'. This did nothing to prevent us getting along absolutely swimmingly.

In the morning Bataa and I set out on bay horses with a third black stallion with a white underbelly carrying my stuff strapped to its saddle across two equally weighted packs. Bataa slung the violin case over his chest like a warrior. My horse (which apparently had no name except 'Mur', which means 'horse' in Mongolian) was much more towards the *zhang tai* end of the spectrum and I could nudge him into a fast trot and eventually a canter. We headed up and away from the two rivers and Bataa immediately began to sing long, rolling melodious songs in a deep and resounding voice.

We crossed small rivers and trotted through valleys and stopped at his brother's ger for lunch after a few hours. Bataa played with his newborn nephew. *Arroz*, a hardened cheese made from yak's milk, was hung up with string around the ger and I ate a piece with my milk tea. At first it tasted like parmesan but then became increasingly bitter, I could barely finish it off and keep a straight face. Another couple pulled up on a motorbike with their young daughter and ate some bread. The wife had an incredibly white face and hands, which seemed very unusual, but there was no way I could try and comment on this without causing confusion and embarrassment, so I didn't.

We rode on and were soon joined by Bataa's dog Aslan. The Mongolian Bankhar breed of dog is an inseparable part of the nomadic herder's life. They are very large, mostly black with brown and white patches, and act as guards to the family encampments – and sometimes as herders of the animals. A common greeting upon visiting a ger is *nokhoi khorio* (hold the dog). I like dogs as much as the next person but these dogs I absolutely loved and formed a strong bond with many I met along the way. Sometimes they were unbelievably playful and I found myself running around with them like a child. Riding a horse is always good but somehow having a Bankhar trotting alongside you completes the experience.

We threaded up through forest and the air became cool and patches of snow and ice appeared. A river cut a deep gash through the mountain rock on our left-hand side. Gold pine needles covered the snowy ground. Aslan kept stopping to root and sniff around but always kept up. We eventually came out into the open and I could see two snow-dusted depressions in the high mountain ahead of us. They sat beyond a snaking river that looked like a sun-bleached pelvis bone. I sure I'd seen this mountain previously in the distance from the Orkhon valley. Bataa's *gers* overlooked this scene on a hill, with his yaks and goats grazing in the river valley below.

We tied up and untacked the horses then sat around the stove with Bataa's wife Chuka, who had a very easy way about her, and ate fresh *tarag* (yoghurt). Propped against the TV was an old, slim bolt-action 22 rifle, that Bataa said he used to kill *chun* (wolf). After we had herded the goats and yaks and tied up the calves for the night, another lady came and sat with us and Bataa insisted I play the fiddle again. I gave them my best Irish jig but they weren't impressed. Chuka mimed without a hint of irony the next day that I should leave the violin with her because such an awful racket would be effective for herding in the yaks in the evenings.

We set off into a cold, crisp late morning but had to dismount as soon as we started to climb the mountainside as it was too steep and icy, and the horses kept slipping. Bataa and I walked up the 45-degree slope leading our mounts and gulping in huge breaths of the icy air. I had four layers on and was pissing sweat under my clothes. We made good time however and walked them down the other side as well just to be safe. Remounting in the next valley, we fell back into the natural rhythm of things. Bataa started singing again, signalling all was well.

We reached a *ger* camp on a hill above Huis Nuur lake. We were now in the Naiman Nuur region made up of eight lakes of varying sizes. We were welcomed into a large *ger* by Dalban, a stout man with huge shoulders, arms and a belly to match, and his handsome wife Miga. Their son, Ochikdurch, oscillated between dark moods of silent broodiness and youthful good-naturedness like a good teenager. Aten Sarne, their pretty 16-year-old daughter was constantly laughing and smiling and had an open spirit. But the undisputed light of the family was three-year-old Onchiksurun, who ran around all day playing and making everyone laugh. We stayed with them for two nights.

Despite the previous evening's woeful performance, Bataa insisted on bringing out my instrument again. This time, however, it was a big hit – largely because I stuck to ballads and let everyone have a go. Dalban and Miga painstakingly handmade delicious *bortz* (meat dumplings) steamed over a simmering basin of water on the central wood stove. Little

Onchiksurun had found some Styrofoam packing cubes from somewhere which we used for a lengthy and uneven boxing match before settling down to some colouring in. I slept in a separate *ger* with a well-stocked burner that cast flickering shadows on the felt-supporting wooden slats of the roof. It was like sleeping in a giant Japanese lantern. I got up in the night to a waxing moon flooding the frozen lake and glistening mountains in its ethereal light. All the stars were hidden from view except … Cassiopeia. "Ha! There you are, you sly witch!"

In the morning the women dressed in thick *deels* and set off to milk the yaks. They sat on tiny stools overlooking the lake and snow-dusted mountains. Dalban and his son let calves out of the pen where they had been secured for the night. He released them one at a time so they would run to their mothers and suckle. After a few minutes, when the milk was flowing, the calf would be tethered to the ground and the yak milk squeezed into a metal pail. The calf was then untethered to resume milking while another one was let out of the pen. It was a solid system. Bataa and I went riding in the afternoon for a few hours across the valley to some other lakes. On the way we saw a family dismantling their ger and packing it onto yaks to transport it down to the valley before winter arrived. Mongolian horses are small but very swift and we cantered them fast over uneven ground whooping like idiots.

That night the family made *shimin arik* or 'Mongolian vodka' – a spirit the strength of a strong wine made from mare's milk. Once the milk has been turned into fermented yoghurt it is heated over the stove with a large tin drum placed around the basin. Within this is suspended a bucket and a second basin of cold water is placed over these. The alcohol evaporates from the yoghurt then condenses into the bucket off the cold basin in a pure liquid. We drank it hot watching Mongolian wrestling on TV and it tasted very much like Japanese sake.

The *gers* had cured goatskins spread out in the entrance-ways. Bankhar dogs lay sleeping curled up or spread out in the sun during the day after barking all night and blanched bones of all descriptions were strewn about the place. It felt like stepping into another time. In the morning Bataa and I led the horses to the lake, cracked the ice and let them drink. We tacked and packed up and then we were off again. It started to snow. Once across the valley we again climbed through another gilded forest.

The going was steep and the snow was thick on the ground. Soft flakes drifted slowly down settling on branches, and the air smelt like ice. The horses seemed to relish the cold and powered up at a steady pace. I gently realised that I felt completely at peace with myself and the world around me. Towards the top it started to get icy and I guided my *mur* over snow or rocks whenever I could. At one section we came upon what looked like a small pond of ice with no way around. "Hmm," I distinctly remember thinking to myself, "I don't like the look of that."

No sooner had this gone through my mind that my *mur* slipped and fell onto his knees. As this happened in slow motion (as these things always seem to), I made sure I kicked out from my stirrups so I could roll harmlessly away to the side and not fall under him. We both scrambled back to our feet and I pushed him onto snow on the other side and got back on. Up ahead I could see that Bataa had dismounted, however, so I got off again and we led our horses up to the icy top where the view opened up to Naiman Nuur. The lake, through the snow, looked like a Norwegian fjord with steep white mountains rising from its edges and a long wooded peninsula sailing through its rippling waters to my right. We led the horses down close to its edge and remounted along the flat part of the trail before we began to climb again. As we did, the snow came in in a whiteout. By this time we had reached a vehicle track with only a few icy patches so we weren't worried.

Both of us were singing as we reached the top (about 2,600m) and all of a sudden, Mogi was there with the parked Hyundi. We had hot coffee sitting inside laughing about the journey, which Bataa was about to backtrack with the horses. Is it madness to pursue such a convoluted journey for one fleeting moment of peace in a snowy forest far from home? Perhaps. But in my experience a person has to immerse themselves in nature for several days or weeks before it can really get to work on you. It takes time for the noise in our minds to declutter and be replaced by the natural rhythms of the earth.

I had assumed my portable solar charger had been either lost or stolen on this journey, but returning the following year with two groups of tourists, the Mongolian family looking after us presented it to me saying I had left it behind in one of their *gers*. It is a great bit of kit and had become an integral part of their lives – every member of the family using it to charge their phones on a daily basis as they have no fixed power source. I found it touching and unbelievably respectful that they had tried to return it to me nevertheless, which I of course refused.

14

ETHIOPIA: HARAR (2016)

J'ai rêvé la nuit verte aux neiges éblouies,
Baiser montant aux yeux des mers avec lenteurs,
La circulation des sèves inouïes,
Et l'éveil jaune et bleu des phosphores chanteurs!

I have dreamed of the green night of the dazzled snows,
The kiss rising slowly to the eyes of the seas,
The circulation of undreamed-of saps,
And the yellow-blue awakening of singing phosphorus!

– Arthur Rimbaud

Harar is undoubtedly Ethiopia's brightest flower. As a jewel, she may be slightly chipped around the edges, though her centre continues to shine with undiminished brilliance. Of course, like most places on the African continent – which Paul Theroux encapsulates as 'a Dark Star' – everything in this town located on the border of the far eastern Somali region is a bit messed up. French-imported blue and white vintage Peugeot taxis cruise beneath Italian-built colonial buildings decked with tropical flowers, giving a strange Cuban twist to Sunni Islam's fourth most holy city after Mecca, Medina and Jerusalem.

The narrow winding streets within the perimeter walls are alternatively whitewashed or painted in pastel shades of blue, viridian, vermillion. While the bitter smell of marijuana smoke is the lifeblood within the fortified walls of Morocco's northern Blue City of Chefchaouen, here it is *khat,* the highly addictive leaf grown on the surrounding plains, releasing an amphetamine buzz when chewed, and occupying the daily thoughts and actions of the majority of the city's inhabitants. Men dye their beards orange. Women wear the most ostentatious, beautifully designed and brightly coloured shammas in the whole country. There are tramps everywhere.

Founded by Sheikh Aw Abadir in 940 A.D., the Harar Kingdom built 99 mosques according to the 99 names of God referred to in the Quran, of which 82 remain today. The four-metre-high limestone wall – or *Jugol* – encircling the old city was constructed from 1551 to keep invaders at bay, although it has often not been successful. The city has been conquered over the centuries by numerous kingdoms including the Adal Sultanate, the Egyptian Caliphate, the Oromo tribe (who advanced through the Rift Valley from the southwest on horse-back, sacking the city before converting to Islam), Abyssinia (under Menelik II), and the Italians.

Harar has historically been one of the main trading hubs between Africa and Arabia, dealing in slaves, principally from the Oromo region (The Prophet Muhammad's wet-nurse is said to have been Ethiopian), hides, coffee, *khat,* ivory, gold, perfumes, incense, musk and salt. Harar's walls were not pene-trated by the Western World until 1855 when British explorer and poet Sir Richard Burton, disguised as a Muslim, entered through the northern gate and stayed for ten days after secretly visiting the holy city of Mecca a year earlier.

I met my guide, Girma, at 8.30am after he had industriously knocked on my door an hour after my arrival the previous evening to offer his services. An ex-radio operator for the Air Force – ("I have jumped from a plane!", he told me) – he served as a young man in one of the many wars with Eritrea and in Somalia. After a delicious breakfast of pancake covered in a thin omelette dipping in honey, we set out to explore to the city. We entered the walls through the southeastern gate – there are five gates corresponding to the five pillars of Islam – and immediately found ourselves in the spice market.

Sheltered by orange tarpaulin, large calico sacks overflowed with anise, cardamom, coriander, dill, mustard, chick peas, lentils, various types of incense, basil, garlic, *khat*, rosemary, oil beans, yellow coffee, *frenjer* (no idea), *abish* (a spice drunk by women after pregnancy), piles of sugar cane and a whole host of other colourful and exotic paraphernalia. The floor was covered with many discarded *khat* leaves. Chatter filled the air in Ge'Sinan or 'Harari', a mix of Amharic, Arabic, Afaan Oromo and Somali only spoken within the city walls.

We continued through winding streets until we reached the governor's house. Ras Tafari, later known as Haile Selassie, was governor of the city in his youth and his old house is now home to an excellent museum. As Ethiopia's last emperor, he renamed the country 'Ethiopia' from 'Abyssinia' in 1963, and is worshipped as a god incarnate among the followers of the Rastafari movement. The name is taken from his pre-imperial name: Tafari Makonnen, with *Ras* – meaning 'Head', a title equivalent to Duke. The Rastafari religion emerged in Jamaica during the 1930s under the influence of the Pan Africanism movement, with Selassie viewed as the messiah who would lead the peoples of Africa and the African diaspora to freedom. With his Solomonic lineage and official titles of *Conquering Lion of the Tribe of Judah* and *King of Kings* and *Elect of God*, he is perceived by the Rastafari as the returned messiah as prophesised in the Book of Revelation in the New Testament: *King of Kings, Lord of Lords, Conquering Lion of the Tribe of Judah,* and *Root of David.* Haile Selassie visited Jamaica on the 21st April 1966 with approximately 100,000 Rastafari from all over the country descending upon the airport in Kingston in a haze of ganja smoke to greet their messiah. This date is still commemorated by the Rastafari as Grounation Day, the anniversary of which is celebrated as the second holiest holiday after the 2nd November, the emperor's Coronation Day.

The coronation of Haile Selassie in November of 1930 was a pivotal event that catapulted the relative backwater of Abyssinia to the forefront of world's attention. British writer Evelyn Waugh's personal account of the event perfectly conveys the uncertain magic and botched brilliance of the country, with the following passages taken from *Remote People,* published in 1931:

> At long intervals the emperor was presented with a robe, orb, spurs, spear, and finally with the crown. A salute of guns was fired, and the crowds outside, scattered all over the surrounding waste spaces, began to cheer, the imperial horses reared up, plunged on top of each other, kicked the gilding off the front of the coach, and broke their

traces. The coachman sprang from the box and whipped them from a safe distance …

It was now about eleven o'clock, the time at which the emperor was due to leave the pavilion. Punctually, to plan, three Abyssinian airplanes rose to greet him. They circled round and round over the tent, eagerly demonstrating their newly acquired art by swooping and curvetting within a few feet of the canvas roof. The noise was appalling; the local chiefs stirred in their sleep and rolled on to their faces; only by the opening and closing of their lips and the turning of their music could we discern that the Coptic deacons were still singing …

In 1935 Italy declared war on Abyssinia and Waugh was sent back to Addis Ababa to cover the conflict. His acerbic account of life as a war correspondent in *Waugh in Abyssinia*, first published in 1936, also captures an important period in the country's history as well as her national character:

The high spirits of the troops seemed unaffected by the weather. In the coming weeks, as the provincial armies passed through the capital on their way to the northern front, we were to see several such displays. For most of the press it was then a new experience. The old chiefs, almost without exception, looked superb. Their gala costume varied in magnificence with their wealth. They had head-dresses and capes of lion skin, circular shields and extravagantly long, curved swords, decorated with metal and coloured stuff; their saddles and harness were brilliant and elaborate.

Examined in detail, of course, the ornaments were of wretched quality, the work of Levantine craftsmen in the Addis bazaar, new, aiming only at maximum ostentation for a minimum price; there was nothing which bore comparison with the splendour of a North African or Asiatic workmanship. But in their general effect, as they emerged from the watery haze which enclosed us, strutted and boasted before the Emperor, and were hustled away in the middle of their speeches by the Court Chamberlains, those old warriors were magnificent.

Back in the Haile Selassie museum, constructed by an Indian architect, the delicate wooden building afforded a good view over the city to the *khat,* peanut, coffee, banana and mango plantations outside *Jugol.* The museum holds various coins found within the walls, including a 12th Century mint from Salahuddin, Maria Theresa silver thalers, and Harari coins, tiny as cufflink buttons, inscribed with no less than 18 Arabic characters. Swords attributed to various kings are on display alongside delicate jewellery, some made with coral brought from the Red Sea. Legal documents and centuries-old copies of the Quran in beautifully flowing Arabic calligraphy line the glass cabinets.

An Italian-made light artillery piece used by Menelik II in his conquest of the city rusts in the courtyard, its Amharic name of *gäräfä* translates as 'the whip'. The museum's curator Abdulahi Sherif explained to me that what was on display is only one fourth of his collection. A friend sat next to him looking rather like an Ethiopian hippy from the 60s with round-rimmed glasses under a sunhat also covering long hair and a straggly beard. Sure enough, just as I was leaving, he said in perfect English: "I am a fan and friend of The Beatles. John Lennon, may his soul rest in peace. See you later alligator."

This just completely stumped me.

We stopped off at one of the blacksmiths' yards where sweating men sat around a furnace powered by an electric fan that whipped up the fire in a kiln to a blistering degree. The men chewed *khat* and used hammers to bang away at plough-tips and axe-heads. Ash from the fire filled the compound. It was like walking into the Middle Ages. Outside, women paraded the streets in shammas of every possible combination of pattern and colour you can imagine. By tradition, only unmarried girls are supposed to wear full silk dresses; married women distinguishable by only the upper parts of their dresses being in silk, the lower in cotton. From what I saw, however, I'm pretty sure that this custom has been metaphorically 'thrown to the wind' with some very married-looking women wearing some very beautiful all-silk-looking dresses.

The acclaimed French poet Arthur Rimbaud arrived in Harar 25 years after Burton in 1880, and, having renounced his huge success as a poet, lived there for between ten and eleven years as the first white trader of coffee and arms in the city, although he never seemed make much money. I had been lucky enough to find a copy of his works in Addis and for a time became engrossed in his tumultuous life story: his lover Verlaine shooting him in the wrist whilst drunk; his feats of genuine exploration in the region; his heart-breaking final letters home as he was carried across the desert in immense pain with a cancerous knee, later amputated, causing his death shortly afterwards in Europe. And, of course, his mystifying poetry interwoven with alchemistic incantations, threads of the occult, colour, light, and magic. Harar was just the place for a man like him.

Rimbaud imported the first camera into the city and on the second floor many of his fascinating prints are on display. I spent a long time looking at them before returning to my room in one of the traditional guesthouses within the *jugol*. All Harari houses are of a similar layout with a large multi-platformed seating area, its levels of seating according to social rank. Colourful plates and wickerwork fill every inch of the whitewashed walls. Wooden beams protrude in a line across the entranceway, the number of rolled-up rugs placed over them indicating how many girls are of marriageable age in the household. Girma and I rested at one of these, while the girl of the house prepared coffee for us.

Harar coffee is considered to be one of the best coffees in the world. Spicy, full-bodied with an almost wine-like texture and taste, Harar beans are some of the oldest still in production. The coffee is naturally sun-dried, the sugars of its red fruit caramelizing and imparting its flavours into the bean itself – a crucial aspect of the overall taste. Ethiopia is the origin of all coffee. A famous story originates from the village of 'Buna', now the Amharic word for 'coffee', in the 'Kaffa' Biosphere Reserve (which is where the internationally recognized word for 'coffee' originates) in the lush jungles of the southwesterly collection of tribes called the Southern Nations, and where we now run coffee tours.

Many moons ago, a goat herder in the forest saw his flock acting strangely after having eaten some red berries from a bush he had never seen before. He collected some of the mysterious berries and took them home to his wife, who cooked them using the wood fire in the centre of their thatched hut. She discovered that if the beans (two half-spheres separated by a membrane inside every berry) were first roasted over a flame and then ground down into powder, they would release their magical properties. Coffee has since spread to be the national drink across the entire country, and is accompanied by the ancient Ethiopian coffee ceremony. Fresh green grass leaves are strewn across the floor while a woman – nearly always wrapped in the traditional light shawl called *netela* – goes through the rather long process of roasting, grinding and brewing the fresh coffee over a fire.

She wafts the smoke from the roasting beans over the brows of her guests, who sit around her on wooden stools, as a blessing. The *buna* is brewed in a large black rounded clay pot called a *jabanah* before being poured into very tiny white porcelain handleless cups, mixed with a veritable mountain of sugar. It is rare for a guest to have less than three cups at a single sitting. Their cup is always dipped in a pail of water before each refill. The coffee ceremony is the central point for so much of Ethiopian community life and, as Sheik Abd-al-Kadir commented in 1587, "Coffee is the common man's gold and like gold it brings to a person the feeling of luxury and nobility."

In the evening Girma and I caught a *bajaj* to the outskirts of the wider city to the rubbish dump at twilight. Here the local hyenas are fed daily and my eyes fixed on them intensely as they emerged from the shadows of plastic-strewn wasteland. They are huge, much larger than a dog, and clearly built of solid, solid muscle. Their long necks protruded forward large grizzled heads, seemingly eaten away in patches around the gums and lips either by dark markings or some terrible disease.

I couldn't tell which. Their slow lolloping gait belies a terrible flashing rapidity of movement. Whoever said that they laugh was lying.

I fed them strips of raw meat draped over sticks along with a few other tourists. I was hazy on the ethics of feeding these wild animals, but truth be told I wanted to see them up close so I went along with it. Although I have to say that once was enough, I found them truly frightening. I thought back to my flippancy as I sat alone, high up in the mountains of Lake Hashinge in 'the floating world' on my previous hike; I had heard the caterwauling of a pack within a couple of hundred metres of me. Although human attacks by hyenas are not common, ignorance can truly be bliss sometimes.

Overlooking the city on a hill, the palatial-looking concrete shell of the country's second dedicated fistula hospital (among numerous fistula centers) was still under construction. A fistula is a medical condition caused by severe or failed childbirth, especially in young girls whose bodies have not yet fully developed enough in order to safely give birth. Holes can develop between the vagina and rectum and bladder, causing a constant leaking of faeces and urine through the vagina. Many women are sexually mistreated in Ethiopia. They can be married off at an unbelievably young age, below even twelve in the very rural areas, with some instances of kidnap and rape whereby they are then forced into marriage. Obstetric fistulas are one of the very worst effects of what can be an unbelievably cruel culture.

The girls and women who are afflicted by this terrible suffering often do not receive treatment, are ostracized by their community and made to live alone in filth, pain and humiliation. The empty shell of the building seemed an appropriate metaphor that although steps are being taken to treat and eradicate this abomination, it is certainly not yet enough. Fortunately, there is the wonderful Hamlin Fistula Clinic in Addis Ababa. It's one of the places we now take YellowWood clients to visit as part of their trip. It has relaxing gardens where the girls and women can recuperate, and even Oprah Winfrey has been there and donated money to build a new wing.

I have never spoken to any of these young women directly with a translator, but I have visited the clinic several times. Peeping inside the wards, many of the girls lie in their beds for most of the day with the sheets pulled over their head, which tells you everything you need to know about the trauma inflicted upon them. But eventually, with much encouragement, many of them begin to come out into the garden huddled together in small groups, warming themselves once again in the sunshine. These sobering thoughts encircled my mind as we walked the outside perimeter of the eastern city walls. Three young girls in matching blue-shaded shammas made their way towards us, laughing and joking with each other, happy and youthfully giggling at the presence of a foreigner. I couldn't imagine anyone, let alone them, being able to deal with such a torture, and more suffering than any person should be called upon to endure.

Towards evening the pace of the city slows to a crawl as most of the men and many women start to really get into their *khat* highs and even the pretence of work is abandoned. Addiction to the drug has caused lots of old men to completely let themselves go, and it's common to find them lumped in filthy alleyways with beads of green saliva spilling down from their mouths. The really old men with no teeth grind the leaves in a mortar and swallow them as a paste. Some of them go crazy eventually. One youngish man had his feet manacled in the street outside his home. Bunches of *khat* leaves in his left hand, he grabbed my hand with his right and wouldn't let go. He spoke good English and seemed well educated, but was clearly out of his mind.

Some of the men are revered for their holiness and Girma was very careful to pick out one man for me to give ten Birr to as an 'offering', although to me it just seemed a money-spinner for more *khat*. A gibbous moon drifted over the city at night to the wails of the muezzins from the mosques. Harar. Crazytown.

15

LEBANON AND MISADVENTURES IN OMAN (2019)

In 2019 I conducted a research trip in Lebanon, which ended up lasting for one month. Later that year I was able to return to guide our first adventure itinerary there for a group of clients, with me again extending my stay for a second month. In the autumn of 2020, following the terrible explosion in the Port of Beirut which propelled the country to the front pages of the world's media, National Geographic Traveller Magazine in the UK asked me to write an article on the country, which is as follows:

Beirut and beyond: why I can't wait to travel in Lebanon again

In the wake of the devastating explosion in Beirut's port in August, Sam McManus, managing director of YellowWood Adventures, reflects on a memorable month-long trip last year through mountains and vineyards — and makes a case for the return of tourism.

Wednesday 21st October 2020

National Geographic Traveller Magazine

Lebanon isn't only the pictures we see in the news. The scene that comes to my mind is one from the spring of 2019. I'm standing at the viewpoint of Saydet el Nourieh shrine, in Hamat, high on a cliff, looking out across the landscape. The turquoise breakers of the eastern Mediterranean meet the coast at the city of Tripoli, after which the land rises through foothills dusted with snow to brooding mountain peaks wrapped in a heavy coat of white. The scene has some of the familiarity of Southern Europe. The traditional houses are made of a solid, creamy stone, topped with orange roof tiles. The woodlands comprise windswept green poplars and Grecian trees with branches like smoke tendrils. Yet all the road signs are in Arabic and the unmistakable dust of the Middle East hangs in the air.

Lebanon is the perfect balance between two worlds, the apex of the meeting point between East and the West, which accounts for both its compelling history and cultural richness — and its turbulence. The first time I went to Lebanon I was supposed to stay for a week but ended up staying for a month.

I was researching whether — and how — to a launch a guided tour in the country. At the time, only a handful of British companies were offering itineraries in Lebanon but its revised and improved safety credentials in the eyes of the British Government Foreign & Commonwealth Office meant there'd soon be more of an appetite. So I took a tiny apartment in Beirut on the top floor of a five-story block with an open terrace, views of the sea and a malicious landlady, and began my research. My time in Lebanon was intoxicating. In November 2019, I'd be back again, leading YellowWood Adventures' first group of clients around the country (and staying on again for a further three weeks, purportedly to observe the pro-democracy protests, but really just because it was nice to be there).

Lebanon is a tiny strip of a country bordered to the south by Israel, with two spines of mountains running perpendicular north to south: the Mount Lebanon range overlooking Beirut and the coast, and the Anti-Lebanon range further east forming a natural border to Syria. Lying between the two, the lush Beqaa Valley houses vineyards and grand chateaus, and feels like France. Here, I explored grand Roman ruins (some of the most significant outside of Italy) of the Temple of Bacchus and Temple of Jupiter in Baalbek. To the Greeks and Romans, this was the bustling ceremonial centre of Heliopolis, their 'City of the Sun', but the streets were quiet. Only the smells of manakish (hot breads served with cheese or zaatar) filled the morning air.

Elsewhere on my trip, my Lebanese friend Milead took me snowshoeing among the cedar forests that crown the head of the Qadisha Valley, which has sheltered

Christian communities since the religion began. 'Qadisha' means 'holy' in Aramaic. And in Byblos, one of the oldest continuously inhabited towns on Earth, and originally home to the seafaring Phoenicians, we ate olives at the legendary Pepe's Fishing Club restaurant, overlooking the port. The menu informed me, somewhat unnecessarily, that the now-deceased proprietor was 'a renowned ladies' man'.

I found Beirut to be both glamorous and high maintenance. In the centre of the city, a beautiful mosque encircled by four minarets stands beside a church with a single tower supporting a crucifix constructed from bright, square lights. Some of the bulbs have blown and the effect always reminded me of the lurid, romantic aesthetic of Baz Luhrmann's 1996 film Romeo + Juliet. At nightfall, the lights from the city give a wondrous shimmering haze to the air, like a finely woven fabric.

Which brings me to the present day. On 4 August 2020, the eyes of the world were on the Lebanese capital as a terrible blast – caused by 2,700 tonnes of inadequately stored ammonium nitrate – ripped through its port. The damage to the city is estimated at £4.6bn, and around 300,000 people were made homeless. In total, 190 people lost their lives. It was a blow upon a bruise for Lebanon, already in steady economic decline caused by a corrupt political system built in the wake of the 1975-1990 Lebanese Civil War. In early 2019, protests against the government brought many local economies to a further standstill. Then came the coronavirus pandemic. Then the blast.

But Lebanon is again rebuilding itself.

Maya Terro, who runs YellowWood Adventures' partner charity, FoodBlessed, is providing thousands of food parcels to those who need it most. In this melting-pot city, there's a rich tapestry of beliefs and communities, but aid is meted out regardless of race, religion, nationality or sex. "We call our beneficiaries 'guests'," Maya says, explaining the intersection of dignity and compassion in their charity. "Now many of the middle class have now become poor, and the poor destitute."

In the weeks following the blast, I also heard from our business partner, Johanna Nader, from Lebanese tourism company TLB Destinations. She's temporarily put aside tourism and switched to mapping the areas of Beirut that most need help, so nowhere gets overlooked. But, she assures me, she's keen to return to her job as soon as possible. "The only industry left in Lebanon is tourism," she says. "The salaries of the janitor in a restaurant to the musician in a pub to the owner of an hotel rely solely on tourism, which helps to bring in foreign currency directly — our local currency has no value anymore." She added: "The Lebanese also need tourism to fall in love all over again with their own country."

I aim to play my part by returning to visit as soon as flights resume and the British government deems it safe, and hope more travellers will join me in 2021 on YellowWood Adventures' tours. Until then, when I think of Lebanon, I won't remember only the shocking images of the recent blast or scenes from the protests. I'll think of the sea and the mountains, and my friends.

"Lots of countries offer clean roads, streets, a bit of history, but Lebanon offers real soul. It's the people all over the country that make this place quite unique," my friend Rana Jabre, a piano teacher in Beirut, told me recently. She's already restored 22 apartments in the city with windows and furniture, with only the help of a friend and carpenter, entirely funded from donations via Facebook. "You know, the cedar trees of Lebanon are mentioned 103 times in the Bible," she said. "They represent resilience and strength because they still flourish in tough conditions. We Lebanese are like the cedar trees."

More info: YellowWood Adventures offer small-group trekking holidays and cultural tours to destinations including Ethiopia, Oman, Mongolia and Kyrgyzstan – plus soon-to-launch hiking itineraries in Romania and north Spain. The 10-day Lebanon adventure costs from £1,550 with bookings available for 2021.

For my first research trip I had managed to book myself onto a group hiking the Lebanon Mountain Trail (LMT), which runs the length of the country. People filtered in and out of the group over the month-long trek at various sections, whom mainly consisted of local Lebanese and Americans of Lebanese decent rediscovering their ancestral home. Two days after flying out from the UK I therefore found myself snowshoeing through cedar forest around the historic Qadisha Valley, overlooking the church of Bcharre that stands like a bastion of faith below a small ski resort, atop cascading waterfalls. From the foot of

Mount al-Makmal in northern Lebanon, the valley is carved by the Qadisha River, also known as the Nahr Abu Ali, which reaches Tripoli before flowing into the sea.

The valley has sheltered Christian monastic communities for many centuries and served as a safe haven against persecution from the Mamluk Sultanate and the Ottomans among others. Lebanon is mentioned 71 times in the Old Testament of the Bible, and its Christian heritage is deeply ingrained in much of the country's architecture, and about one third of the nation's psyche. We spent a night in a beautiful stone auberge, watching a pink sunset descend upon the glittering snow. In the nearby restaurant that looked like a country kitchen, I and my hiking companions drank red wine from the monastery below in the valley and ate vegetable soup from hand-fired clay bowls.

In the morning some of us sat in the back of a pickup truck and whizzed through villages watching the mountainsides fall away to the ocean in the distance whilst the sunlight danced on the road. We met an entrepreneurial nut proprietor selling a vast array of nuts and dried fruits from the trunk of his car. The Lebanese I was with were cold towards him however, because he was Syrian and would allegedly not put the money he made back into their economy, but rather only spend it amongst other Syrians. Since the start of the Syrian Civil War in 2011, millions of Syrian refugees have fled into Lebanon, and it has been estimated that over 1.5 million of them still reside there, which equates roughly to one Syrian refugee per four Lebanese nationals, although this is changing all the time.

The spring was late and the snows still heavy as we stumbled our way down into the cedar reserve, often falling in the deep snow. It was very peaceful and still. We were eventually consumed by cloud so we had to retreat to another auberge just outside of Tannourine where we huddled around a huge log fire protected by a heatproof glass plate, before I hitched a ride with one of the guides back to the capital. I took a tiny apartment in Beirut on the top floor of a five-story apartment block. It was monastic in its dimensions, only alleviated by a single window of crumbling periwinkle blue wooden shutters that let in every mosquito, and an open terrace comprised of the large open roof of the apartment below.

The latter had views of Colombian-looking white tower blocks protruding from the green bushy mountainsides to the east, and a sea view only partly obscured by a modern hospital to the west. It came complete with a malicious young landlady who complained to me loudly about all the tenants, including a very old man who ran the corner store, whom I found to be softly spoken and gentle. I spent many a happy evening sitting on my terrace eating tomatoes of varying sizes brought from a vegetable stall along the street, laden with hummus and raw onion. Sometimes life converges at a single point where you just know there is nowhere else you would rather be. I still had to keep up with running the business of course, so I would walk down the many terraced steps of the hilly city to the neighborhood of Mar Mikhael where I had found a communal office space that always had plenty of coffee and people to talk to.

On the way small bars and restaurants overflowed onto the city steps where young men and women smoked incessantly and seemed to be talking about important subjects. I'd pass a barbershop where men leaned their heads back to have their stubble razored. One of the patrons cracked a smile at a joke, and I saw his gold tooth twinkle in the sunlight, and made a mental note that I should remember this piece of 'local colour'. Beirut has some fancy modern districts, but the backstreets are by far the most interesting. The graffiti is imaginative and artistic. Lots of beautiful trees and plants entwine the stone pillars of the old stone buildings. Many people own fancy cars they can't afford. On one motorcycle below the back seat was stenciled: 'Grass, Gas, or Ass – No One Rides for Free'.

My Lebanese Christian friends would criticize the Muslims for having too many children in this tiny and already overpopulated country. The Muslims I had the chance to speak with mainly consisted of cab drivers who were unable to escape my torrent of mispronounced Arabic, although I didn't (and couldn't) ask them about how they felt about the Christians. Whatever the social tensions, no one ever wants to revert to the blood-letting of the fifteen-year civil war (1975-1990) however; where Christian fought Muslim, Christian fought Christian, Israelis, Syrians, Druze, Palestinians, and a million people fled the country.

I went on a day-hike with Rana, a friend of my Arabic teacher in London. After the constant noise and bustle of the city, it was a relief to return to the peace of a small mountain pass. It was called 'The Place of the Dead' because (according to my hiking companions) pilgrims had been murdered here on their way to Damascus, both in ancient and not so ancient times. The snow was heavy on the ground here too, and after tying some plastic bags around the trainers of a young under-prepared woman hiking with us to prevent her feet from getting wet, we descended down a gentle slope leading to abandoned terraced fields with dilapidated dry-stone walls. Thousands of butterflies were migrating north and the air was filled with them dancing around us.

We reached a very old and rich mountain village called Douma, where the traditional Lebanese stone houses were very large and grand with thick stone balconies protruding from the windows over the main street. We looked in a shop selling many varieties of olives before stopping in the square for some orange juice. Some children were playing on bikes and Rana asked to have a go on one of them so I requested the smallest pink bicycle from a five year-old girl, and somehow managed to ride the tiny pedals around the square to squeals of delight and laughter around me.

In the Beqaa Valley I was driven past some small Syrian refugee camps of tied down tarpaulin. I was travelling with a faithful 86-year-old taxi driver called Joseph. We stopped to drink a beautiful bottle of red wine at Chateau Kefraya's outdoor restaurant, in the shade of woven grass mats suspended over a pergola. Our attempts at communication were so bad that the family next to us couldn't stop themselves laughing, so they joined in our conversation for an hour or so – an example of so many spontaneous exchanges that happen every day in Lebanon. I awoke the next morning with a splitting wine head-ache after a great night out in the nearby mountain town of Zahle, that had involved a hard-drinking Japanese from the Red Cross in Iraq, a lost and found credit card and two very beautiful Lebanese women that no one slept with.

I made my way to Baalbek, located to the east of the Litani River, close to the Syrian border, and had a shawarma in an overpriced café talking to a highly educated man called Jihad.

I paid for my ticket to enter the incredible temple ruins, only to lie down immediately and sleep for an hour in the sun. Back down on the Mediterranean coast, there is a tiny island just eighty metres off from the coast of Sidon, the third largest city in Lebanon, with a history that dates back to 4000 BC. In Phoenician times the island was the site of a temple to their god Melqart. This was later turned by the Romans into a temple for their gods, and they cut huge circular pillars of grey granite to house their idols.

When the Christian Crusaders came, they laid these pillars flat as horizontal structural foundations for the castle they built on the island, and you can clearly see the grey granite circles evenly interspaced between the sandy rock constructs of the fortress walls rising from the sea. When the Crusaders left, the Mamluks built upon the castle, and after them a small domed mosque was constructed, whose origin is probably Ottoman, known as *Masjed Qalaat el Bahr* [Mosque of the sea fortress]. The mosque is a simple cubic form topped by a central dome. Small groups of the Muslim faithful will have laid out their prayer rugs inside and bowed to Allah over the ruins and bones of so many who have done so before them to their own gods. Such is Lebanon: dilapidated, rejuvenated, holy.

But city life isn't for me, and after a few consecutive weeks in Beirut I decided to fly to Oman on a wild camping trip, to also scope out an itinerary there for clients. I had purchased a tiny pathetic excuse for a tent in a gun shop in Beirut, and was adamant that I was going to camp my entire stay of about a month. It wasn't my first time in Oman, as when I lived in the neighbouring United Arab Emirates I used to come camping here regularly. It is one of few countries in the Middle

East that I would consider safe enough to do this; such is the good-natured friendliness of its people.

My friend Hamel once lent me his bright red Porsche Carrera and I had driven down from Dubai to Muscat with my girlfriend for a night in what I had then dubbed 'the city of seduction'. This time, when I landed in Muscat's new cavernous airport, I went straight to the car rental company desk, then up an escalator to the top floor of a carpark simmering beneath a hot sun, and drove my unimpressive KIA Sportage (all they had left after a run on their 4x4 rentals) unthinkingly into the maze of spaghetti tarmac that encircles the city like a cheap doily, blindly following the Satnav and trying not to crash.

I had a couple of meetings in Muscat that day with some local tour operators, and after these had finished, I headed down the coast to find a place to camp, armed with a new Oman country guide filled with highlights and their satellite coordinates. My plan didn't work, however, as by the time I pulled into a gas station it was getting dark and I was so exhausted I had to park nearby and sleep for a few hours in the car. I eventually reached a beautiful small stretch of coast that smelled of fish, but couldn't find anywhere to camp so spent the night sleeping in the car with the driver's seat pushed right back, getting bitten by mosquitoes whining through the salt air, and listening to hens scratching in a nearby homestead. I was just too tired to care.

In the morning I drove to Wadi Tiwi and when the road narrowed I set off on foot into the winding valley with plenty of fresh water in my backpack. The contradictions of Oman's natural environment are difficult to capture because of their acute diversity: in this *wadi* [valley] the chocolate-reddish-orange stone of the high peaks gave way immediately to a lush green fertile strip of palm trees, tall grasses, crops, bushes, flowers and orchards hemmed in by grey stone shingle of river pebbles like a Japanese garden. The road was of a light doughy concrete scarred by linear markings to help the grip of tyres. I plodded up a steep incline past maroon walls of private yet humble houses.

I was out of shape after the fleshpots of Beirut, but the bite of familiar muscles felt good as did the pull of the lungs going deeper than of recent weeks, knocking free the pollution of the city. Palm fronds hung seductively over the road, framing picture postcard memories. I walked on sweating without really knowing where I was going. Reaching the natural end of the valley there was a village and an enterprising Omani showed me the way down through terraced mountainside shadowed by tall wet palms to where the river cut dramatic formations into the valley rock. A group of city Omanis clad in rented wetsuits were taking an abseiling lesson. It was a nice spot.

I befriended a black American guy called Koketso who lived in the nearby coastal city of Sur, and we walked back together sharing anecdotes of Middle East expat life that come easily to the initiated. He showed me the best Indian restaurant in Sur and insisted on paying for the meal as I was his guest, as is the custom. The restaurant had an add-on hotel next door with good wifi so I stayed here a few days working from the hotel lobby drinking coffees and camping on the white sand beach. Sur is famous for its Arabian *Dhow* boats, still made in their timeless graceful design from timber and sail. Camping on the beach I could see amorous couples walking along the promenade in the lamplight, yet I was content in my solitary world among the small fishing boats upturned in the sand.

I continued driving the next day over a suspension bridge as a *dhow* lazily sloped beneath me out the estuary towards the briny ocean. Three now useless stone castle turrets adorned the mountainside in picture perfect symmetry, remnants of the time when a bullet from a *jezail* was the law of this land. I followed the tarmac road through a moonscape topography and dropped into a turtle sanctuary before striking camp in some wretched spot. I followed the deserted coast round the curve of the easternmost point of the Gulf peninsula and now I was driving west along the southern coast with a view to reaching the port city of Salalah, close to the Yemeni border.

I'm not sure I passed another car on this stretch of coastal road. The sea skulked on my left beyond rolling pale gold sand dunes. These same dunes drifted away to my right in an undulating sea of endless waves like a bad special effect from an 80s sci-fi movie. Large globules of sand had audaciously spread themselves over the tarmac on either side of the road, making me swerve around them as if walking through a party of playing children who aren't to be minded. My unthought-through plan to drive to Salalah rapidly receded when I parked next to a camel in the twilight of dusk at the jumping off point to the island of Masirah, and saw from my map that I had only covered a quarter of the distance in a full day's driving. 'No one is going to want to do that,' I thought to myself, and headed north again.

But before I would find myself back in the cultural heartlands of Oman, I first had to cross the sunbaked orange sands of the Wahiba. As my Korean 4x4 entered the sandy ruts of a well-used desert road, I saw a Jeep Wrangler pass by me in the opposite direction with its roof smashed in, clearly due to being rolled down a sand dune. The Omani driver poked his head out the window so he could see past the smashed windscreen, his white teeth flashing in a very pleased-with-himself attitude as his dishdasha flapped in the wind.

Britain and Oman have always shared a strong diplomatic relationship, not least because Oman has been the historic port of call for the trade of arms (notably the Martini-Henry rifle) into the Gulf, of which Britain are willing suppliers. The legendary British explorer Sir Ranulph Fiennes served in the army in Oman from 1968-1970, aiding the Sultan in his skirmishes with the Marxist-indoctrinated guerrillas in Dhofar, the treacherous territory in the south bordering Yemen (previously known as 'Aden' at the time of the British Empire).

I recalled an extract from his excellent account of his time fighting here, *Where Soldiers Fear To Tread*: "Two thousand years before the Persian hordes who invaded Oman found the heat so great that the jewels fell out of their helmets and the feathers from their arrows." (Two months later, I would meet Sir Ranulph Fiennes at London Olympia at the Adventure Travel Show, where we were both giving talks on our respective misadventures. This historic meeting took place at the urinals in the toilets where we were standing next to each other. I had of course read that he had had to remove some of his fingers due to frostbite, but was naturally hesitant to actually look over and verify this.)

Fortunately, now there are some well-run desert camps in Oman. I introduced myself as a tour operator – a well-made weighty business card goes far in most places I have found – and was promptly given an exhaustive guided tour of the facilities, situated in the sandy valley between towering perpendicular kilometre-long sand dunes. The tour concluded in the main seating area of a permanent tent housing an enormous hand-woven carpet upon which rich Omani children ran around amusing themselves screaming. I greedily helped myself to some dates and bitter coffee.

I didn't want to drive back just yet, so I took some water from the car and started walking up one of the soaring sandy walls of the natural valley. I was gassing and sweating buckets the whole way up, and at the top I threw up the dates and coffee, such was the strain of 'two steps up one step back' in the loose sand under a merciless sun. But the view was worth it. I followed the snaking curves of the ridge of a dune, where there were no footprints around of any kind, to the top of a peak of sand to where the camp far below was obliterated from sight. My eyes settled on the dreams of Arabia: endless, clean waves of soft golden sand. Not littered with pylons or bits of old tyre like in the UAE, they appeared how they had always been.

Driving back along the sandy road I was starting to feel like I was getting the hang of things. Hesitation can be fatal; you must pick your line through the sands and just go for it at speed. Natural ruts are formed and you can follow these for a while but they never last. The more I trusted my judgement, the more it paid off. Like many things it just takes a bit of getting used to and I was enjoying it with gusto. I got back onto the tarmac and after a minor detour getting lost along some backroads of a nondescript town hanging onto the edge of the desert, I headed back north towards the mountains.

I drove for a long time and as it began to get dark I began to tire and then suddenly I was completely exhausted and realised that driving any further was now dangerous. I could tell

I was coming into a city of some description which was the last thing I wanted as I was adamant on my non-hotel policy for this adventure. I suddenly saw a neon-lit sign for 'Travel Agent' by the side of the road and pulled off to ask them for a campsite. Two Indian gentlemen were seated at a large desk and I asked them where I could camp. They gestured to a dark patch of nothing on the other side of the motorway and this was as good as I was going to get so I made the crossing and drove into the darkness.

After a while I pulled off the road in somewhere where there were no lights which felt secluded enough. I put up my pathetic tent, unrolled my sleeping mat and sleeping bag, stripped down to my underwear in the baking heat and lay down on the bedding in a mental fog of exhaustion. Just as I was dropping off, I was awakened by the lights of a car highlighting the interior of my tent. A driver had obviously seen my camping spot from the road and pulled off for a closer inspection. This was far from ideal, especially as I had no idea where I was. The car eventually left, but I was now spooked. Clearly, I was exposed and this dark patch of road was more frequented than I had hoped. But suddenly a plan came to my sleep-deprived befuddled mind; if I parked my 4x4 between my tent and the road no one would see me and just think it was a parked car and I would be ignored – perfect.

I unzipped my tent and skipped out deftly across the sand in my underwear with visions of the actor Richard Burton scaling the wire in 'The Spy Who Came In from the Cold', such was the cunning of my little foray into espionage. Yet just like the unfortunate character Alec Leamas, no sooner had I sat in the driver's seat and turned on the engine, the interior of my vehicle was flooded with the full-beam searchlight of what I sensed to be a Toyota Land Cruiser (I was correct) which had again pulled off the road to interrogate this unwelcome trespasser in foreign lands. A stalemate ensued. There I was, poised in my underpants, highlighted under the full beam of the Nazi guards, with my head on the steering wheel cursing my luck.

In truth, even in that moment I couldn't help but see the funny side of the situation, although of course I didn't know how it was going to play out … I quickly realised my number one priority was to get some clothes on. The stalemate continued. There was no movement from the car; no doors were opening, and I was still bathed in light and all my clothes were in the tent. There was nothing for it – I opened the driver's door and strode out Bold As Brass in my pants to my tent where I hastily pulled on some clothes then without skipping a beat I strode over to the Toyota loudly shouting the customary welcome greetings in Arabic.

As soon as I came up beside the Land Cruiser my adrenaline dipped as I could tell that the five Omani men seated in the car in white dishdasha wearing rounded ornately woven circular caps with shining rounded flecks of mirror embraided into the design were not of a malicious nature. They were as perturbed about me as I was about them. In the ensuing confusion of Arabic and English laid forth from both sides, it was concluded that I could not camp here and they would show me to a more suitable spot as they owned this land and it was too close to their house (there was no house in sight). I was in no position to argue and packed everything back into my car and followed them a kilometre down the road and camped in an identical stretch of barren desert close to the road where I remained unmolested for the rest of the night in the deepest of sleeps.

A lot of driving and a few minor adventures eventually brought me to Jebel Akhdar [the green mountains] which I explored for a few days. One of my favourite places is Oman is the ancient village of Misfat Al Breyeen, nestled at the foot of the mountains of the sun. I parked alongside a couple of vans laden with German and Swiss tourists emptying out to see the town, which at first made me uneasy. But, like the Himalayas, when something is worth seeing you cannot begrudge others wanting to do the same. Walking under the terraced date palm fronds along the tinkling waterways of the *falaj* irrigation networks, I quickly lost the crowds, however, and sensed the ancient feeling of calm.

I lazily followed a path up towards a mountain valley out of the village. Two Omani boys came bolting past me chasing a donkey on the loose. I started chatting to two young Omani men I met on the path, clad in the pure white dishdasha, but with their heads bare. One worked for a local oil company and the other was in the army. They were cousins. The man in the army was married and the other – more portly than his cousin – was 'looking for a woman'. We befriended each other in an easy way and spent the rest of the afternoon together exploring the beautiful plantation of this hidden oasis.

We headed back to the stone-built town and were invited for coffee and dates by a local headman there. He refused payment of any kind from any of us. I kept looking under sofa cushions, over balconies and under coffee cups for a women for our oil-worker friend (his iPhone was full of pictures of Omani women) which had everyone laughing. Sometime later I was driving down one of the steepest mountain roads I have ever navigated. It led to Wadi Bani Awf or 'Snake Canyon', which dissects the souring Hajar Mountains to the west of Muscat in a deep rift, and is popular with tourists for canyoning.

I eventually reached the pebbly valley of the riverbed and parked up, glad to still be alive and using my feet like God intended. I took off my shoes and waded into the waist-high waters of the canyon through two perfectly vertical walls of rock. It looked like the entrance to some hidden kingdom of Middle Earth. The canyon is very difficult to traverse and tourists should never enter without a qualified guide. It forked as soon as I emerged from the long narrow straight pool of water. I chose the right-hand fork and ambled up the unpredictable terrain of fallen boulders through which weaved a gushing river, deep pools, trees, bushes, scrub, vines, shingle and rock. After a short amount of time an Omani man and a white male German tourist approached me, and I could tell something was wrong.

The Omani told me that a German woman had broken her ankle "badly" about 40 minutes up the canyon. They didn't have a phone which I found incredulous. I gave them mine with my local Omani SIM and he called for a mountain rescue ambulance. I also called a local tour operator in Muscat we now use, and they informed me that there was no helicopter access in the canyon and that the 4x4 ambulance coming from the capital wouldn't arrive for an hour at the earliest (and they would still have to climb up and bring her out).

I figured we still had another 90 minutes of daylight. I wasn't worried – the ambulance and professionals were on their way and I was sure the guides would get her down in time. The Omani and German tourist sped back up the canyon ahead of me whilst I made my way up the canyon at a more leisurely pace. I was still sweating however as it was heavy going. I remember thinking that it would be interesting to see how a mountain evacuation was conducted here. When I reached the group the scene that met my eyes was of a vastly different nature however.

The lady was in a wetsuit like the rest of the group, and supposedly being carried by four Omani men, sitting on their interlaced hands, but they just weren't getting anywhere. They had moved her a total of 20 metres in the last hour and she was now freezing cold and shivering. The foot connected to the broken (shattered) ankle was still in its trainer and was flopping around like the head of a drunk, causing god knows what further damage. A handful of mainly Indian tourists also in wetsuits were scattered around, completely unused to the difficult terrain and barely able to look after themselves. I very quickly realised this woman was in very real danger of death from hypothermia and shock, and would almost certainly die if she didn't get out of the canyon by nightfall. We had about an hour of daylight left.

Before heading to Lebanon, I had attended a refresher outdoor first aid course near Poole in Dorset (UK) at the behest of Cathy, our Head of Operations at YellowWood. The scenarios acted out in green fields next to ambivalent cows now kicked in. I removed the lady's shoe, made a splint from two strong pieces of wood lying about and secured the foot and ankle with a strong bandage. I still felt like the guides could get her out but after a further ten minutes when it was clear they couldn't move her, and it transpired that they were not in fact qualified guides, I just put her on my back and walked her out of there.

My dad was a paratrooper for many years in the British Territorial Army. When I was a child and we faced a difficult situation, he had always repeated the phrase: "It's good training", although exactly for what was never made clear. I have therefore derived a bizarre pleasure from carrying loads far heavier than needed on my hikes around the world, and this phrase again came into my mind at this moment, and I smiled to myself. Honestly, after all those heavy rucksacks it was no bother; I just carried her out of there for about forty-five minutes and put her in her car. Her friends said thank you and gave me an orange, and as I walked back I saw the 4x4 ambulance coming with blue lights flashing in the twilight. I waved them in the direction of her and then went to sleep in my tent pitched over some rocks in the valley, feeling useful.

16

ETHIOPIA: THE BALE MOUNTAINS (2016)

Within minutes of my bus journey into the heart of Oromo country, I was immediately taken with the people. They were even friendlier, amidst a friendly country, than all of the people on all of my bus rides. And I had taken a lot. A few words of Arabic were an instant hit as it is widely spoken by the largely Muslim community here. As soon as we started to enter the mountains I also realised I was in terrain that demanded appreciation. It was beautiful in the peaceful, Zen-inspiring way of the foothills and mountains of Kyushu, Japan; lush, verdant hillsides punctuated by soft grey boulders. 'Ah', I thought, 'this is my kind of country.'

The Sanetti Plateau in the Bale Mountains is 'The Rooftop of Africa', averaging 4000m in altitude, it is the highest plateau on the entire African continent. Located in the south of the country, the plateau eventually drops down to the mysterious Harenna cloud forest, where wild coffee grows, and lions and wild dogs roam all the way to the Kenyan border. Approximately a six-hour drive down from Addis, I hopped down from the bus in the one-road town of Dinsho calling goodbye to my new-found friends: *"Kabullala, ashoufkom bikhair."* [May all of your prayers be answered, see you in goodness.] I walked down the road in the crisp mountain air to meet some acquaintances I had contacted via email a few months previously.

I met with Ayuba, a local mountain guide, and Matt, a former Peace Corps worker with three years of experience in the region, now working for the Frankfurt Zoological Society; both were influential members of the Bale Mountains National Park community. We went to the 'London Cafe' a medium-sized room where the local men congregate to drink bottled water and chew *khat*, and after talking for an hour or so I left them in search of food. I was promptly invited to a local restaurant by Dr. Endalkaehew Birhanu, a veterinary surgeon universally referred to as 'Doc', and Warekei Tadesse, also a local guide of the region. Both could speak excellent English, which was most appreciated as yet again I was in a new region that spoke a completely different language.

We drank beer and ate roast meat and after I ordered a round of *arake* for everyone things rapidly started to get loose. We ended up five grown men dancing in the bar wearing straw cowboy hats we had taken down from the walls, only stopping for swigs of neat gin; after half a large glass of *arake* each we all manfully agreed that 70% proof is just too strong to be taken in quantity. Doc had a very endearing laugh, making his entire body shake with mirth, and he became a human vibrator for most of the evening. Warekei was a proficient dancer despite his ample girth. He led us in numerous jaunts to local songs, which left all but him gasping for air at the end of each rendition. A priest insisted in buying me two bottles of beer before we all eventually stumbled back to our relative homes under a canopy of shining stars.

Awaking with a rather sore head, I realised I had work to do. Gurbinder Kundi (Binder), a Corporate Treasurer and long-time friend in Dubai, had been hinting for a while that he would be interested to come out and join me for a leg of my trip, and we had subsequently arranged for him to partake in six days out of my ten-day trek across the Sanetti Plateau. Due to the nature of the terrain and the fact that I was now catering to the needs of someone other than myself, the trip needed some significant preparation, especially compared to my usual style of 'turn up with a backpack and see what happens'.

With the help of my local contacts I procured a guide, a cook, two horse-handlers with three horses to carry supplies and equipment, ten-days' worth of provisions, a minivan to pick up Binder from the forest-town of Rira for his journey back to Addis to catch his flight, and sufficient funds from the bank in the next town. After completing all of the permits at the park office we were good to go. Binder has a lot of experience working in Africa so I didn't have to worry about him reaching me; I just pointed him in the right direction of the bus station and before I knew it the next evening we were eating roast meat in the very same restaurant as my previous 'dance-off'.

We set out the next morning to walk across the rooftop of Africa. Having loaded the horses, we headed up into the grasslands just outside Dinsho. Binder carried a daypack but I insisted on carrying my full pack through a combination of habit and stupidity; "It's good training." We were immediately surrounded by an abundance of exotic wildlife. Male and female mountain nyala walked amongst small herds of redback deer. The male nyala, larger than a British stag, have graceful slender curving horns that rise straight up towards the sky with an air of regal nobility. The females are without horns but have the same daintily cupped ears, like the curvature of a leaf designed to catch water, giving them an inquisitive, superior aspect. This, combined with the soft white and grey markings on their fur, make them the most gracious of creatures.

These herds were interspersed with the huffing, grunting movements of large warthogs, their tusks curving out and around from their snub noses. I unsuspectingly came across one at very close quarters in the tall grass and it bolted just in front of me with surprising speed. We crossed the single tarmac road laden with Anubis baboons and headed up at a steep incline into the forests of the mountain range on the northern flank of the plateau. Ancient lichen-covered monoliths with peeling orange trunks soared above us in a tangle of vines and creepers, and then we were up and out onto a sunny pathway traversing the ridge where the vegetation thinned to large expanses of short grass interspersed by masses of 'everlasting flower', a deciduous bush that grows in densely packed clumps like silvery rock formations.

A collection of three male mountain nyala emerged from a wooded thicket onto an open expanse. As I approached them they bolted, their large limbs throwing up small clods of earth as they comfortably navigated a small ridge, disappearing from sight. Binder and I strolled along in high spirits, led by our guide, Jafer Mohammed, the head of the Bale Nyala Guiding Association. I estimated him to be in his fifties but was not so bold enough to enquire. He was a dignified and thoughtful man, and I immediately placed my trust in him, which was at no point unwarranted.

He may or may not have heard us role-playing particular exchanges between the Jafar the evil vizier and his talking parrot Iago from Disney's *Aladdin* – "Patience Iago, patience!" – and was either too dignified to acknowledge them, or just simply baffled at the juvenile idiocy of two men in their thirties. We reached camp in a valley filled with everlasting flower. The horse-handlers had taken a direct route from Dinsho and had already set up our tent while Usman Abdullah, our cook, had fresh coffee brewed awaiting our arrival. It was accompanied by an aluminium dish of mixed *kolo* [roasted barley] and peanuts.

We lounged about in the sun on our roll-mats snacking on this and boiled halves of potato dipped in salt and Tabasco sauce. This satisfying starter was followed by huge platefuls of penne pasta in a spicy tomato and vegetable sauce, topped off with sweet mugfull's of hot tea. I immediately realised that I had been conducting my trips in entirely the wrong manner, vowing on the spot to never travel in Africa again without an entourage of at least five. My notion was confirmed the next day as I awoke to the sound of Jafer's voice calling us. "Binder, Sam, breakfast is ready!"

'Oh yes', I internalised, 'this is how you do it'.

Two mugs of *buna* and two freshly baked chapattis dipped in fresh spicy *shiro* bean curd later, we shouldered our packs and headed west down into the flatlands encircling the plateau range. The lowlands are the habitat of the endemic and endangered Ethiopian Wolf and we saw several of these solitary hunters crossing the dusty plain, their glossy red fur catching the sunlight. After a relatively short walk of four or five hours we reached camp at Sodota to find our tent pitched next to the Ethiopian Wolf research station cabin there. They are truly beautiful animals, foxlike and rather playful-looking in appearance, you forget that you are looking at an accomplished predator.

There had unfortunately been a recent epidemic of a disease transmitted from the dogs of the local herders to the wolves, which had tragically wiped out a large percentage of their population in the previous months. I later spoke with the head of the Frankfurt Zoological Society, who are doing as much as they can to save the remaining wolves, and he explained that they had managed to vaccinate a small number of them in time. The presence of herders pasturing their livestock in the park causes other problems including erosion. Twelve million people in the surrounding area depend on the water run-off from the plateau, which acts like a giant sponge for rainwater, and the erosion caused by 10,000 or so herders is affecting this supply for all these people. It is an on-going issue that requires government attention.

I was still full of beans after we reached camp and saddled up one of the horses to go for a ride. Our horse-handlers were Abdullah, a large man with huge hands and feet and the countenance of a 'gentle giant', and Haji, smaller and permanently clad in a blue bobble-hat giving him the likeness of an Ethiopian Noddy. Haji explained to me, through Jafer, that horses in Ethiopia are named according to their colouring. Our three stallions where therefore named *Odocha* – 'white and black', *Adi* – 'white' – and *Dama* – 'brown and red'. In Bale only male horses are used for riding and luggage transport, the females left to raise their young in the fields.

You only ever mount from the right-hand-side of the horse in this region, so I accordingly hopped up onto Dama. I stuck to the track as there are many mole-rat holes on the plain, and took Dama through a trot, to a canter then finally into a short gallop. It felt great to be out alone in the midst of such vast empty spaces. I hauled him to a stop and sat for quite a long time staring at the undulating hills in the distance, feeling the soft breeze on my face. The horses in the park and the sur-rounding area are large, sturdy beasts and beautiful to ride. I was very pleased to see how well they are treated, with no or extremely limited markings of trauma from over-heavy loads.

Abdullah and Haji were both highly competent horsemen, literally having grown up in the saddle, and it was lovely to have Dama, Odocha and Adi roaming free around our camp-sites, occasionally lying down and having a good roll in any particularly appealing dust baths. Back at the camp one of the station researchers, an Ethiopian, had unlocked the door of the cabin and Binder and I sat inside on cowhide sofas with our feet up chatting about this and that. Outside tiny moorland chats hopped around picking at the dirt daily cleaned out from the mole-rat holes. It is a symbiotic relationship as if the moorland chat is present, the mole-rat knows there is no immediate threat from predators.

One fat and rather ambitious little chat hopped in to the cabin entranceway while we were eating dinner at the table, and we fed him some breadcrumbs. He was shortly joined by his friends and some yellow-breasted Abyssinian longclaws. In the morning Jafer called us excitedly and we ran down to the plain where a family of four wolves were making their way north, often stopping to play amongst themselves, and we were able to get up quite close. We then began our ascent up and around the western side of Sanetti and it felt good to make some altitude. We spooked several wild hares, each bolting with incredible speed, and camped about halfway up by a natural cave created by a huge boulder, where Usman built a fire for cooking. The boulder was beneath a large ridgeline running for about 300 metres some height above us. The line was comprised of rock formations averaging about six metres high, resembling the stone statues of Easter Island. It was like camping below an army of sentinels. Binder and I climbed up and onto the highest sentinel to watch the saffron orb of the sun gently dip through the valley we had walked up that day.

Usman, Abdullah and Haji rolled out a rug facing Mecca to the northeast, and in a neat line bowed down and prayed. That night the temperature plummeted at around midnight and we were both glad we had brought good sleeping bags. The next morning we were right up in the grasslands of the plateau, everlasting flower giving a silver sheen with hints of azure to the rolling hills. We could feel the air thin and were afforded an amazing view across the entire western plateau to the mountain formations in the distance, broken in layered contours like ploughed earth. The sentinels of our camp had only been a foretaste of what was to come as our path led us past a huge gorge crowned on all sides by what Jafer called 'the stone forest'.

It stretched for miles and truly resembled an alpine forest, the only difference being that it is was entirely of free-standing smooth rock formations that twisted up in bizarre, unpredictable shapes. Walking in and around them, we headed in a southwesterly direction until we were delighted to find that our camp at Rafu was set amongst the formations, our tents pitched in the middle of small rock circles. A woman with two young children was staying in a very large grass-thatched hut nestled amongst the stone trunks. Binder, Jafer, Usman, Haji, Abdullah and myself sat around a fire in a smaller grass hut next to a dung-fenced goat corral. The woman gave us fresh cows milk as a gift of hospitality and we drank it with our coffee.

Binder and I decided to walk up a nearby hill to see the view. The long expanse of the steppe revealed itself with shadows cast down from the atmosphere gliding across the pale flaxen tableland. Facing south, the plateau plummeted down in front of us for a thousand metres in heather-clad mountainsides leading to golden barley fields, groves of giant bamboo and the lichen-covered Harenna Forest. To the west, layers of peaks and ridges backed up in ever watered-down rows of colour until they became indiscernible from a fat sky, pregnant with cumulonimbus clouds resting in billowing heaps. On our way down Binder played some music from his phone and just as the sun threw out its last shards between the giant lobelia and the mind-bending stone forest in front of us, Led Zeppelin's *Stairway to Heaven* came on the playlist. No more perfect song could have better fitted the scenery.

In the morning, light flooded through the opened tent flap, framing a view of Dama grazing. Setting off for the day, we entered the jungle town of Rira through countryside dotted with houses constructed entirely from bamboo fronds, the weaving tapering up to form flimsy points; the locals were effectively living in giant baskets. We sat by the roadside and ordered sodas as being a Muslim village they sold no beer. We continued on past a mosque constructed entirely from corrugated tin sheets, and another twenty minutes down the road we had reached our campsite, which was a relief as it was very hot now that we were down from the highlands.

We were aware that we were rather dirty and so headed down to a nearby stream for a good wash. Finding a lovely little number trickling through a pasture, we followed it up to where a small waterfall afforded a natural shower beneath a large tree covered in spider webs. We stripped to our underpants and took turns scrubbing ourselves with soap and splashing in the refreshing water. Back at the campsite we sat on the soft grass in the evening sunlight, chatting the night away with our companions and a local scout manning the area for the government. Jafer told us that Binder was the first person of Indian heritage (his only word to describe an Indian person was 'Hind!') that he had ever seen walking in the mountains. In the morning the three of us ventured into the bamboo forest and sat beside large shady rock pools, watching ten-metre high waterfalls gush down into them.

On the way back to camp we crossed the river that leads to the waterfalls and found Usman and Abdullah washing their clothes upstream from two young girls, involved in the same occupation. The girls were cooking some form of inedible sour apple in a vat over a log fire as when cooked the apples make an effective soap. The girls used their feet to work the lather into the family blankets amidst much giggling and snatching of glances at the two foreigners. I'd had the unprecedented foresight the previous day to call Ahmed, Binder's driver, and ask him to bring us eight cold bottles of beer. When we reached camp we saw that the minivan had already arrived and we sat on the grass drinking the cold suds watching three horses being driven round in a threshing circle in the barley field next door. It was Valentines Day and it seemed not a dreadful way to spend it.

Binder and I said our goodbyes after lunch, and I figured that now was as good a time as any to try some *khat*. Usman brought a load from the village and the six of us, including the scout, sat in a circle on the grass. Abdullah briefly left to the stream to fetch some water and upon his return said that he had received a call from home informing him that his wife was unwell and potentially having a miscarriage at five months pregnancy. He refused assistance and left immediately to the village to catch a bus. I saw him later in Dinsho and although his wife had indeed lost the child, she was not herself greatly physically harmed, which is no small blessing in a remote area. I had made sure he was fully paid for the time he missed due to this tragic occurrence.

Although all feeling bad for Abdullah, there was nothing we could do to further help him so we returned to our circle and palaver. One simply chews and swallows the *khat* leaves amid sips of water to clear your mouth out. Although not extremely potent in its effects, I gradually felt a compelling feeling of elation combined with a strong clarity of thought, and enjoyed speaking with Jafer at length on a number of topics. We had dinner, after which I had a small stomachache, and I awoke late in the night and was unable to get back to sleep, which is apparently one of the common side effects. Emerging from my tent in the night, the stars of the Milky Way sprawled across the sky in a glittering mass, a half moon illuminating the pale fields.

In the morning Jafer and I set off up the road to climb back into the highlands. Haji and Usman followed shortly after as soon as the horses were loaded, our party of six now reduced to four. Following the winding track up we passed a group of Colobus monkeys jumping between several large trees. The black and white markings of their faces gave the impression they were wearing a Cardinal's hat; one male sat watching us in religious repose on a high branch, his long slender tail with its bushy white end hanging down.

We stopped for a short break in the shade between some giant heather trees and a young man with an Islamic-style beard, shaved at the front but left to grow thick around the chops and chin, walked down the track towards us from the other direction. He knew Jafer and the two men chatted in Oromo while I, for lack of anything better to do, sharpened his plastic-handled machete with a sharpening stone I kept in my pack. Just as we neared the top of the climb the horses caught us up and we all sat together eating chocolate spread lathered over chapattis in the sunshine, playing on our phones.

Our supplies having dwindled, only two of the horses now carried the luggage and Usman and Haji took turns in riding Odocha. In direct contrast to the natural abundance of the valley we had just come from, back on the plateau there was an eerie silence, broken only by the whistling of the wind. We made for the lee of a towering mountain of rock, a couple of grass huts huddled around its base, and camp was struck as soon as Haji confirmed there was good water in a nearby stream. We were at the foot of Tuludimtu, the highest peak of the plateau and the second highest of the country.

It was supposed to be another three days back to Dinsho from this camp but I ruined everyone's plan by heading up to the top alone as it was only mid-afternoon and *it was just right there*. Hopping over the stream I picked my way through the boulder-strewn landscape on a faint path that led up in a long arcing curve to the summit. Towards the top I could really feel the thin air and was breathing very heavily. There is a small telephone station perched on the pinnacle with numerous cream-coloured satellites fixed to the steel mesh of a tower. I could tell that Jafer had felt guilty in my going alone and he had said that he would phone to check on me.

At the top I realised that my phone battery was just about to die and knew that he would worry and probably even come after me if he couldn't contact me, so I laid my folding solar panels on a rock with the cord plugged into my phone. The satellite station is always posted with a guard on a five-day rotation and the current poor soul on duty came over to greet me. He had on a large ALASKA beanie hat with a scarf hung over his head beneath it and down each side looking like long ears. He had no front teeth and somehow resembled a friendly teddy bear. I also had my hand-held steady-cam-mounted video camera with me, which does not look unlike a laser gun. I had a strange little Star Wars moment to myself, reasoning that I must just be tripping on the altitude somewhat.

Saying that, the view around me was from another planet; beneath a cobalt sky, light flaxen shades touched with olive, azure and rust spread out all around me, shadows from fast-moving clouds drifting across them at pace. It was barren and beautiful and I felt a pronounced sense of calm. Jafer called and I let him know that I was fine and would head down in an hour or so. My teddy bear friend turned on his box radio which proceeded to blare out national songs, most of which I knew and was now thoroughly fed-up of, so I moved away from him and walked around the satellite station looking at the views on all sides.

It felt like the end of my journey. I would never be able to top this. I also missed having my friend around to share it with. I spent what may have been an hour lost in thought, more feeling the place than observing it, basking in the far-reaching perspectives that mountains afford to life. I said a final farewell to the vastness and headed back to camp, each step now a return compared with the odyssey that had preceded them.

In the morning, as Jafer and I skirted the southern base of Tuludimtu heading east, a sea of cloud nestled right up to the table's edge in plumes of fluffy cotton wool bedding, the valley of Rira now completely obliterated by the wispy mass. Regardless of a strong wind whipping at our faces, the skin drying out under the sun's undiluted force, I just had to see the cloud line from a little higher up and asked Jafer to wait in the shade of a large boulder while I clambered halfway back up the mountainside to take in the whole view. After dropping down a little from a long walk over the cloudland, we passed our initially planned campsite of Gebre Garacha [Black Water], a huge windswept lake of Atlantic blue and had our lunch there instead.

We then continued our route march northward with a lot of ground to cover and Jafer setting a fine pace. We stormed across a wide alpine valley of grass and everlasting flower, small peaks on either side and straight ahead, culminating in the perfect pyramid of Wassama Mountain. It felt like a cross between Switzerland and the Lake District, only lifted up on stilts, floating on cloud, in Africa. We reached camp after about three and a half hours with no break. We had both kept a good pace and enjoyed the march but upon arriving the adrenaline stopped and both of us felt tired. Jafer curled up in a thick *gabi* next to a fire that Usman had built in a natural cave (he and Haji had taken a shortcut with the horses skipping the lake) and I dozed in my tent for twenty minutes.

A young girl from a family of herders staying up above us brought us cow's milk and Jafer and Haji joked with her as she had never seen a foreigner before. We gave her a hot chapatti covered in jam but I don't think she liked it much. The stars shone brightly as we all sat around the fire in the lee of the cave, smoke occasionally drifting into our eyes. On the long decent to Dinsho the following day I realized that we had gained the plateau via something of a side stairwell, as the northern approach was open and large and you could see everything.

As the mountains of Sanetti receded behind us in a crown of tussling watercolour peaks, lesser mountains and scenes of pastoral bliss presented themselves. We walked through many settlements with much harvesting of barley and horse thresh-ing. One farmer holding a small curved sickle knew Jafer and joked for him to come and help. Trees appeared again and chil-dren played around streams trickling through soft pastures. We were back in the world. I had met an Italian gentleman called Luigi in the Gheralta Mountains who has lived for many years in Ethiopia. He bought me an excellent lunch one time, and afterwards when we were talking he had said: "You know, if you really want to see this country you have to get off the roads. You have to walk through it on your own two feet. Your own two feet!" He wasn't lying.

I spent some time in the nearby Southern Nations eating

fried fish and watching hippos at lake Awasa but the bulk of my trip in Ethiopia was over and I knew it.

Whereas previously I had found the capital, Addis Ababa, claustrophobic and dirty, upon my return now I revelled in its diversity, craving again the luxuries of modern civilisation: some friends and I went to dinner at the best Italian in town called Castelli's – we knew it was the best place in town because there is a framed photo of the proprietor and his wife gawping next to Angelina Jolie and Brad Pitt – and we had spaghetti in a truffle sauce and linguini with saffron, and drank good red wine. I went to watch a band of African musicians from all along the Nile play instruments I didn't understand. I sat in the garden of the oldest hotel in the country drinking macchiatos, writing in the shade of a tree. I took taxis when I knew I could have taken the metro. I had spaghetti with cream and spinach for breakfast.

But in the quieter days, as I cast my mind back over my journey, I realised the country had, slowly and imperceptibly, reignited a small golden flame in my chest that I had carelessly allowed to become smothered, starved of oxygen and finally extinguished altogether by the waxy layers of our modern life. Here it had once again continued to burn with an ever-increasing strength as the days and miles past, until once again it was a roaring furnace. I felt the wings of the human spirit once again stretched wide, and life flooding down through my very arteries. I was alive.

17

EPILOGUE: COSTA RICA – A CASE STUDY OF ECOTOURISM (2020)

When the COVID-19 pandemic came in early 2020, it was obvious that I was going to have to put my business on hold. I did what any self-respecting travel entrepreneur would do in this situation, and jumped on a flight from London to Costa Rica arriving two days before the country's borders closed. It was a gamble. No one knew at the start of the pandemic what was going to happen and I don't mind admitting that my first night in a hostel in San Jose was a rather sleepless one. Fear was in the air and I very much felt like a lone salmon swimming against the current of the tourists literally fleeing the country.

The next day I stood on the ferry as it pulled out towards the heavily-jungled Nicoya Peninsula on the Pacific coast. I saw a squadron of pelicans swoop down from a 'Jurassic Park' volcano backdrop, and glide unsteadily over the silvery water, and I knew I was going to be okay. I spent five months living by the beach in the small town of Santa Teresa, surfing nearly every day in the glistening ocean. It was the longest I'd stayed in one place in as many years. I made friends with amazing people, all of us thrown together and living through an uncertain time. Completely immersed in nature, I was able to slow down, rest, reflect and study. I needed this time more than I realised. I felt with great certainty, much like I had in Cairo five years previously standing before the statue of the negro Nubian Pharaoh, that another sea-change was coming on.

I had done a lot of rushing around, building, searching for meaning and new experiences since I'd first set out for Ethiopia five years previously. Now I needed to step back and allow myself time to pull my experiences together, to forge more profound connections and a steadier direction. In the mornings, surfboard under arm, I would walk beneath the high cathedral of the canopy above, its lime green light streaming down as howler monkeys tightrope-walked along the black power cables following the dirt road, whooping as their large testicles swayed from side to side. Armoured iguanas clattered up thick trunks as I passed them by, before heading out onto the golden sand and plunging into the crystal waters.

With Nicaragua to the north and Panama to the south in Central America, Costa Rica is a thin green strip of tropical rainforest and volcanoes that rise up between the Pacific Ocean and the Caribbean Sea. Its human population is a little over five million, and it is one of the most biologically diverse places in the world due to its unique geography and the many resulting microclimates, which allow for a vast array of ecosystems. It has become the poster child for sustainable ecotourism throughout the world. With a quarter of its land under the protection of national parks or reserves, the country has become a world-leading example of how linking tourism with a growing protected area network can lead to the simultaneous growth of both its socioeconomic and environmental sectors. The country's journey to this point is a fascinating one.

José Figueres Ferrer, the son of Spanish parents settled in Costa Rica, was a well-educated, prosperous coffee grower and rope manufacturer, but his criticism of the government of Rafael Angel Calderón Guardia in July 1942 forced him into exile in Mexico for two years. He then embarked on a political career, founding the Social Democratic Party upon his return, which eventually led to him becoming a revolutionary leader, culminating in the overthrow of Costa Rica's government via civil war. When he became provisional president of Costa Rica in 1948, he abolished the national army, nationalised its banking sector, granted women and Afro-Costa Ricans the right to vote, guaranteed public education and a host of other decrees which set the country on a path to prosperous stability, subsequently making it an increasingly popular tourist destination in the region.

By sheer dumb luck I was staying in the surf town of Santa Teresa, which happens to be located right next to Cabo Blanco Absolute Natural Reserve on the southern tip of the Nicoya Peninsula. This unbelievably beautiful and wild reserve was the first nationally protected area in Costa Rica, established in 1963 by Karen Mogensen from Denmark and her Swedish husband Nicolas (Olaf) Wessberg, both examples of the steadily increasing influx of international tourists. With the aid of an international agency, they bought 1,250 hectares of land on the peninsula to protect it against the local farmers who were deforesting huge swathes of rainforest to feed the international demand for beef, causing soil erosion, loss of soil fertility and decimating wildlife populations, including many rare and endemic species.

Nicolas was later tragically murdered in 1975 whilst spearheading the conservation of the now established and equally beautiful Corcovado National Park on the more southerly Osa Peninsula, and Karen died in 1996. Yet their legacy remains to this day. Both witnessed the first national park of Santa Rosa, established in 1972 in the northwest of the country – the first of now 28 national parks. As with much of human history, Costa Rica's progress towards developing a national system for ecotourism was long and complex, combining many factors, successes and setbacks. Yet the overarching principle was that as more tourists visited, more wilderness was set aside for protection, as the government could clearly see this is where the long-term economic benefit lay.

Costa Rica's National Park Services was created, and by 1998, all the natural reservations were organised under a national system. Costa Rica was popularly deemed as the leading ecotourism country in the world, which attracted more tourists in a positive feedback loop model; whereby conservation efforts protect the natural environment whilst also generating healthy economic results, creating in turn both direct and indirect employment, contributing to a reduction of poverty. Tourist numbers steadily increased from 329,000 in 1987, to 1.03 million in 1999, over 2 million in 2008, and 3.14 million tourists in 2019.

A number of systems have been put in place help manage the impact of this increasing footfall including the Bandera Azul (blue flag) programme which promotes development while curbing the negative impacts of mass tourism. It assists local communities to work against pollution and protect the environment by evaluating the environmental quality of coastal areas, and awarding them a number of stars. The voluntary Certification for Sustainable Tourism Programme (CST) encourages businesses to become sustainable in a variety of ways, including using recycled products, implementing water and energy saving devices, properly disposing and treating waste, conserving and expanding Costa Rica's forests, in a way that can be measured and publicised. Millions of trees are planted every year as a result, and the tree coverage of the forests across the country have literally doubled in the last 30 years.

The model also has a positive effect on the lives of the local people. The country continues to face some challenges such as income inequality and some of the darker sides of the tourism industry such as sex tourism, but as models go it is pretty fantastic. Costa Rica again came first in the Happy Planet Index rankings in 2020 which measures how well nations are doing at achieving wellbeing and long, happy, sustainable lives of its populations, having previously come top in the 2009 and 2012 rankings also. By 2015, the country was also able to produce 99% of its electricity from renewable sources, and the government continues to invest in renewable energy generation in an effort to meet its goal of becoming carbon neutral by 2021. According to the non-profit Borgen Project, the majority of this energy, 67.5%, comes from hydropower, with wind power generating 17%, geothermal sources 13.5% and biomass and solar panels comprising 0.84%. The remaining 1.16% is from backup plants.

Costa Rica's eco-tourism experiment offers a path to

recovery for the rest of the world.

Over the past years nearly every single local guide we've used to lead groups through mountains, forests and deserts has commented to me on the changing and increasing unpredictability of weather patterns, and I can see the effects of global warming for myself, increasingly both in person and via the global media. I am not ahead of the curve, but I am on the curve, and am doing what I can to help protect what Carl Sagan called our 'Pale Blue Dot'. Christiana Figueres, daughter of the previously mentioned three-time president José Figueres Ferrer, was the former Executive Secretary of the United Nations Framework Convention on Climate Change.

She was a key architect of the 2015 Paris Agreement. This is a legally binding international treaty on climate change adopted by 196 Parties at the 21st session of the Conference of the Parties to the United Nations Framework Convention on Climate Change (COP 21) in Paris, on 12 December 2015. Its goal is to limit global warming to well below 2, preferably to 1.5 degrees Celsius. To achieve this long-term temperature goal, countries aim to reach global peaking of greenhouse gas emissions as soon as possible to achieve a climate neutral world by mid-century. The Paris Agreement is a landmark in the multilateral climate change process because, for the first time, a binding agreement brings all nations into a common cause to undertake ambitious efforts to combat climate change and adapt to its effects.

This historic agreement also coincided with the establishment of the 17 Sustainable Development Goals (SDGs) at the COP 21 in Paris, to end poverty, protect the planet and enable a path to prosperity for all. The SDGs are increasingly becoming integrated as a global language that institutions can agree upon, and work towards. Christina Figueres published a book in 2020 with co-author Tom Rivett-Carnac entitled: *The Future We Choose: Surviving the Climate Crisis*. I would encourage you to read this or listen to it as an audiobook, as it lays out the steps we can each take in our daily lives to help achieve the goals of the Paris Agreement.

For my part, I wish to continue to use adventure travel as a medium to help promote sustainable practices in countries across the world, and to educate our clients on their importance. Adventure travel is still faced with the 'elephant in the room' conundrum of the international flights clients and guides need to take to reach some destinations, and the resulting carbon emissions these produce. While we may indeed have green hydrogen-powered planes in 30 years' time, in the meantime we will continue compensating for these carbon emissions by planting trees via our partner charity WeForest, in Ethiopia, Brazil, and other countries.

More than just aiming for carbon-neutrality, however, we can do far better by actively contributing to the regeneration and rewilding of the environments we visit, by partnering with local conservation organisations that use versions of the model laid out by Costa Rica in other countries around the world. For our adventure itineraries we partner with conservation charities in the countries we travel in, and are seeing this as a welcome growing trend across fellow travel companies. This is an opportunity for the adventure travel industry to financially support conservation in destinations around the world, reduce its overall carbon footprint, and engage travellers in the world's climate issues.

If our itineraries are more culturally focused, we partner with philanthropic charities, to help the vulnerable in the communities we meet, such as the Fistula Clinic in Ethiopia, for example. By using local suppliers for accommodation, meals, transport and guides, funds will also always find their way into the local economies.

Imagine if Brazil adopted a fully sustainable ecotourism model to replace the current insanity of hacking away the Amazon rainforest – one of the great lungs of our planet – for the short-term and unsustainable profits produced by cattle ranches and palm oil plantations. The amount of carbon sunk in the earth by reducing then reversing this deforestation, funded by the channeling of proceeds from tourism to the rewilding and the protection of biodiversity by the local communities, is the kind of economic model we need to promote and achieve if we are to all survive the climate crisis.

In May 2018 Former US Vice President Al Gore said: "The world is in the early stages of a sustainability revolution, that has the magnitude and scale of the industrial revolution, at the speed of the digital revolution." The COVID-19 pandemic which began in 2020, has instigated an unforeseen benefit of significantly increasing the pace of this change. Many governments around the world are seriously considering how best to reduce emissions with a view to avoiding catastrophic climate change, while continuing to grow their economies. Some have begun to implement policies to achieve their goals, including setting a number of 'net-zero' targets.

This trend has been encouraged by the rapid development and falling cost of clean technologies, and the rapidly increasing interest from global investors in ESG-compliment

(Environmental, Social, and Governance) and sustainable asset classes. Combined, this momentum in policy, technology, finance and the growing awareness of the climate crisis in mainstream culture for many populations, has affected an ever-growing list of sectors, with energy transition investment and sustainable finance flows hitting new records in 2020. So, there is certainly hope.

A human generation does not last long in the grand timeline of humanity, and humanity hasn't lasted very long thus far in the grand timeline of the planet. So hopefully it won't be long before the changes we are going through now will just be contemporary history, and our descendants will look back on us as antiquated apes who insisted on burning fossil fuels to move around the place, keep warm and watch TV. A general shift to 'back to nature' can only be a good thing. The stories in this book will become dated very quickly, but some of the feelings they describe will not. Because when you go to the wild places of this earth and tap into the undercurrents of nature that continue to ebb and flow there, it is very clear that they haven't changed at all.

Sam McManus, Asturias, North Spain, 2021

Sam McManus, Asturias, North Spain, 2021

In partnership with:

Yellow Wood
Adventures

yellowwoodadventures.com